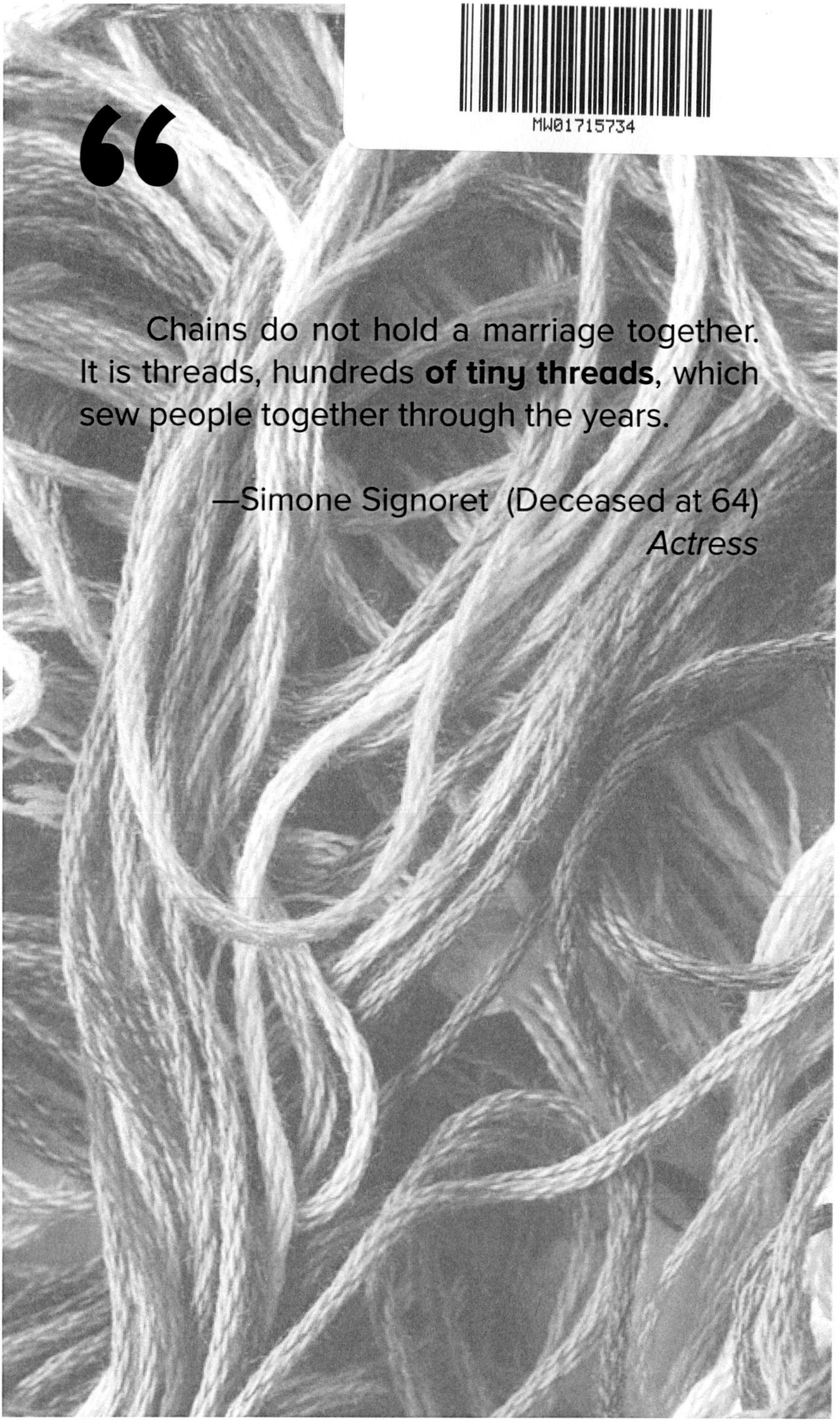

"

Chains do not hold a marriage together. It is threads, hundreds **of tiny threads**, which sew people together through the years.

—Simone Signoret (Deceased at 64)
Actress

of **TINY THREADS**

[STORIES] *about* American Marriage

[edited by]
Jess Hagemann

CIDER SPOON STORIES | FORTY ACRES PRESS

Cider Spoon Stories
Austin, Texas
www.ciderspoonstories.com

Interior design by Cider Spoon Stories
Cover design by Tiara Marshall
Printing by Forty Acres Press
Manufactured in the United States of America

[for]

David & Emily Tietz

If I ever get married, I want a relationship like yours.

CONTENTS

Note: To the extent that the interviewees' stories have been edited to fit this book, they were modified as faithfully as possible in keeping with the original dates, places, sequence of events, etc., as relayed to Jess Hagemann between September 2016 and March 2018. Some names and other identifying details have been changed to protect privacy. Others are used with permission.

INTRODUCTION

The 1933 film *The Ex-Lady* (directed by Robert Florey and starring Bette Davis) was notable for its time in three respects. Its plot revolves around an open marriage; the wife in particular is forward-thinking, brash, and holds remarkably similar views to today's Millennials;[1] and the fairly revealing negligees that Bette Davis's character wears slipped in after the Motion Picture Production Code had been adopted but before it was in force.

It's a great film—one that I watched in preparation for writing this book. Like its title suggests, hundreds of individual fibers (quiet moments; arresting philosophies; times for speaking and owning and loving and letting go) went into researching, compiling, and publishing the tapestry that is, finally, *Of Tiny Threads*.

Unlike Books I and II in the *Untellable Tales* series, which each took approximately a year to complete, this project, Book III, took two years. It required more extensive groundwork—more questions, with more abstract answers—than either *Postmarks on Our Foreheads* (2016) or *Whispers* (2017) before it, as I struggled first to understand my own feelings about marriage, then to reconcile them with the burden of

---

1 According to a 2017 U.S. Census Bureau report, "Most of today's Americans [aged 18-34] believe that educational and economic accomplishments are extremely important milestones of adulthood. In contrast, marriage and parenthood rank low: over half of Americans believe that marrying and having children are not very important in order to become an adult." https://www.census.gov/content/dam/Census/library/publications/2017/demo/p20-579.pdf

choice in the land of the free.[2]

Thirdly, I hoped to isolate a cross section of project participants that could at least begin to represent the diversity of preference and experience influencing marriage today. One book can't tell every story, but *Of Tiny Threads* tells eleven of them, easing if not erasing the oft-dividing lines of age, orientation, race, culture, and religion.

Here is marriage in America today. Here are the choices that people have made; the partners they've made them with; the particular joys and the universal challenges that other couples (and thruples) can look forward to, already know intimately, or should take to heart ... as words of caution if not promise; as tales of true love and false hopes; convenient legal commitments and spiritual contracts that transcend time and life itself; lovers who wanted it so badly it hurt; and lonely (or regretful) hearts who didn't want it to hurt anymore.

Their stories come as-is, off the rack: in vivid color and with the occasional flaw, revealed in snapshot, held up to the light without judgment. There are many

---

2 As Aziz Ansari notes in his brilliant *Time* article "Everything You Thought You Knew about Love is Wrong," single Americans have everything laid out before them, and no clear direction to follow. They either don't bother trying, or end up experiencing 'paralysis by analysis'—overwhelmed by the sheer number of mate choices now readily available on dating apps like Tinder. "Throw in the fact that people now get married later in life than ever before, turning their early 20s into a relentless hunt for more romantic options than previous generations could have ever imagined, and you have a recipe for romance gone haywire," he writes. "The stunning fact remains: it was quicker for my dad [who had an arranged marriage] to find a wife than it is for me to decide where to eat dinner." http://time.com/aziz-ansari-modern-romance/

threads that make the marriage garment—not just something old, something new, something borrowed, and/or something blue.[3]

My own story is not included among them. At 31, I've yet to become engaged or say I Do—making me an Old Maid by 1970s standards, but par for the course in 2018. In the 1970s, 8 in 10 people married by the time they turned 30. Today, not until the age of 45 have 8 in 10 people married.[4]

I used to believe that I would never marry. Why would I? Educated and financially independent, I didn't 'need' a man to get me out of my parents' house the way that women really did in the past. I was happy alone. (Or maybe I didn't like compromising? And I assumed 'compromise' and 'sacrifice' were synonyms for 'marriage.') Anytime I was in a relationship, the thought of 'legitimizing' it in the eyes of church and state seemed silly and outdated. *Okay, you get a tax break. And maybe God won't send you to hell. Big whoop*, I scoffed.

Then my literary hero Elizabeth Gilbert wrote *Committed* (2010), a (mostly negative) treatise on mar-

---

3 In case, like me, you wondered where that little rhyme comes from: well, "something old" represents continuity. Insofar as the human race must procreate (barring some freaky but not impossible medical advancements) if the species is to continue, "something old" provides protection for the bride's eventual baby. "Something new" offers optimism for the future. The "something borrowed" should come from a happy wife, symbolizing the transfer of luck from one bride to another. "Something blue" stands for purity, love, and fidelity—though it might also ward off the evil eye. https://www.msn.com/en-us/lifestyle/weddings/heres-the-real-meaning-behind-the-something-old-something-new-wedding-rhyme/ar-BByUIVF

4 https://www.census.gov/content/dam/Census/library/publications/2017/demo/p20-579.pdf

riage that largely reinforced my beliefs. (Though her sociological portrait of the institution across time and cultures probably inspired this book in no small way.)

And THEN I dove headfirst into the interviews for *Of Tiny Threads*. While I'd like to tell you I've been completely cured of my cynicism, I still maintain that marriage is not for everyone—but perhaps it's a more viable choice than I ever imagined.

If I had to isolate one theme or 'lesson' that emerged during the interview process again and again, it was that marriage is not the wedding day. It is not a 'one-and-done' event on the road to Happily Ever After. It requires choosing the same one (or more) person(s) every hour of every day. It's less about Gilbert's idea of being "committed," and more about recommitting, with gusto, regularly.

Equally, marriage is about knowing when it's no longer the right path for you—or when it was never your vocation to begin with.

Simon's* marriage works because he and his long-time wife sometimes 'look the other way' when it comes to acting on their baser impulses or emotional whims. Beth* and Sandy* lived together for over 40 years, before finally tying the knot in their 60s. Jade* and her partner have consciously decided never to marry—but to remain monogamous all the same. Jenna* and Adam*, two Millennials, just celebrated their second wedding anniversary, and here reflect on the first two years. Julie* and Prabin*, both of Indian origin, had a semi-arranged marriage—voluntarily.

Morgana* and Devin* decided to marry 100 times in 100 ceremonies. Reigh* and Katie* fled the U.S. to escape queer persecution. Ellen's* husband, a businessman who prioritizes work over their marriage, has blessed her liaisons with another man. Sheila's* marriage is rooted in a shared spirituality. Robert* doesn't know how long his marriage will last. Triad members Lindsay* and Hannah* are both 'married' to Samuel*, and they're raising one child among the three of them.

In between each chapter, marriage 'soundbites' capture overheard conversations, solicited remarks, film and literary quotes, and bits of longer diatribes. Divorcees A.M.* and Michael* explain how divorce affected them and their families. Dari* spills the secret to a long-lasting marriage. Toni* reflects on marrying her soulmate in a traditional Yoruba ceremony.

Finally, in two special sections, therapists Brendan Owens and Dr. Allison Sallee shed light on the most common issues that couples face, and share what Austin nonprofit C2 Change is doing to help.

If you're overwhelmed, intrigued, put off, confused, or grateful ... read on. We have everything to learn from those who have been there, done that—are doing it—whether you've been married fifty years or you plan to enter a convent. I've pulled aside the curtain for you. Please silence your cell phones and come in.

—Jess (31)
30 JUNE 2018

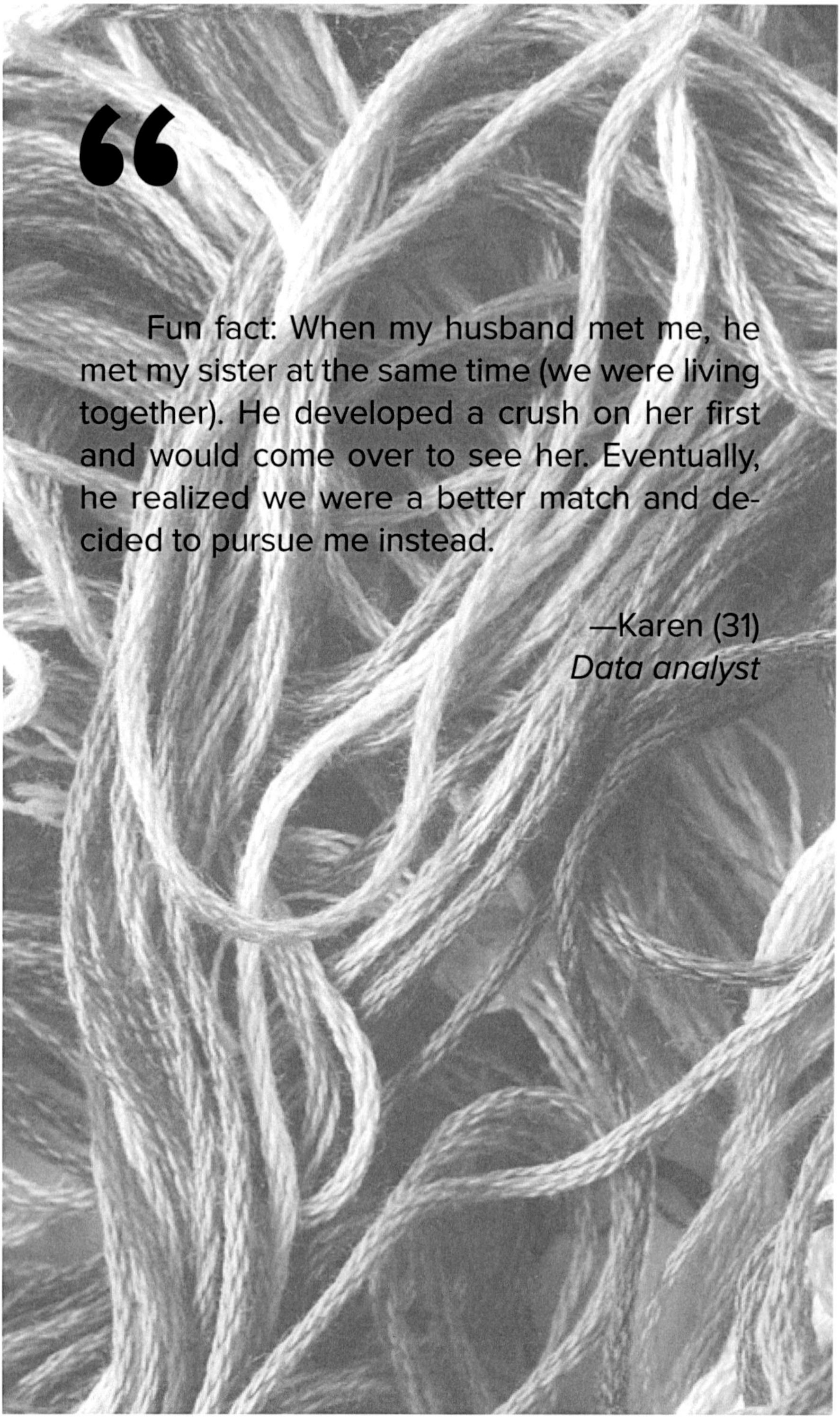

“

Fun fact: When my husband met me, he met my sister at the same time (we were living together). He developed a crush on her first and would come over to see her. Eventually, he realized we were a better match and decided to pursue me instead.

—Karen (31)
Data analyst

SIMON & CHRISTA

[Simon (50) is a conflict resolution specialist in Austin, Texas. It was Simon's experience with family relationships and reconciliation that I thought made him especially qualified to comment, as a sort of prelude, on the marriage relationship in general, and on his own marriage in particular—as Simon and wife Christa have what some might call a 'monogamish' marriage.]

New Trends in American Marriage

The idea that the ideal, mature relationship is one in which you find and marry a person of the opposite sex, then satisfy each other's needs in every area for the rest of your lives, 'til death do you part, happily ever after, yada-yada ... it's just not true. Certainly not for 100% of people and certainly not when it comes to lifelong relationships, where both partners are (hopefully) always evolving and changing. I mean, it happens, I'm sure, but it's probably pretty rare, and so you see a couple of things happening in American society today.

First, divorce. Divorce is legal in this country and there's not the stigma around it that there used to be. There's not even much stigma around multiple divorces. It's like people have decided that there's a time in life when having one partner in a stable relationship is very important, and that time usually corresponds with child-rearing. From the time a kid is born to the time he leaves the house, the partners try really hard to stay together—but before that, there's cheating, and after that, in the 'retirement phase' of life, when the kids are gone and it's just you and your partner, then there's no shame in saying, "You know, it was a great run while it lasted, but it's just not working for me." And then they either get divorced, or one or both start cheating again. They cheat because they have needs that aren't being met, and they've put the burden of responsibility for meeting those needs squarely on the shoulders of their spouse.

The second thing that's happening—and we're seeing this more and more now—is people who decide the whole marriage thing isn't for them and they're not even getting married. Women especially have more economic power now; they don't have to get married to support themselves, so many choose not to. Or they choose divorce for the same reason: *I can afford to make it on my own, so why stay married?* Other couples swear up and down that they're partners for life and don't need the institution of marriage to prove anything, but then they end up splitting anyway because there's not the hurdle of a legal divorce complicating their decision.

The only factor influencing those people's decision to 'go their separate ways' is if a kid has resulted from the relationship, as then the state has to get involved anyway. Maybe they never married to avoid the scrutiny of the state, but now the government wants to know how that child's being taken care of. Regardless of whether the parents were ever married, both parents have a legal obligation to make sure the kid's not out on the streets: he's got to have healthcare and education and all of that. Deciding to have a kid, or to marry someone who has a kid, changes the equation. Minor dependents add a whole new level of responsibility and accountability. Basically you'll be interacting in some way with your co-parent for the rest of the kid's life, whether you're married to them or not. In that sense, children (rather than the legal institution of marriage) are the glue of many marriages.

Then there are the people who talk about having 'starter' marriages. "Oh, we didn't have any kids, we just share a cat; we didn't even buy a house, so, you know ... " It's like they're 'practicing' for the next marriage, which will be the 'real' marriage—but the odds of marriage #2 working out better than the starter marriage aren't any better, and are in fact probably worse. I think most starter marriages are entered with good intentions. Young people have the romantic idea that because they've found a romantic partner, and everyone is happy for them, they should make that person The One romantic partner and get married. Or they belong to a culture that proscribes sexual intimacy before marriage, and they're ready to be intimate. Still other young people are like: *Marriage is the last thing we need to prove that we love each other.*

I call my wife, Christa, my 'first' wife as a kind of joke. An homage to starter marriages, if you will. We've been married 30 years and she's my first and only wife, which makes us an anomaly among our friends. Most of them make it 10 or 12 years with their spouse, then a fraction of them get divorced, and another fraction remarry. When we all get together for parties it takes 15 minutes to introduce everybody and get the relationships straight. Here's my first wife, here's my second partner, here's my son's mother, etc. Christa has picked it up, too. She calls me her 'first' husband, but she's quick to clarify if somebody asks that "Yeah, we're still married."

So, people are doing all sorts of interesting things: they're waiting to get married; they're never getting married; they're married to one person but have various relationships with other people (either spiritual, emotional, or physical relationships). Sometimes the partner is completely in agreement; other times, it's more European—where the guy ends up having a mistress on the side, his wife kind of knows, but as long as he doesn't spend a lot of money on her, or a lot of time, everybody goes along with it.

Men aren't the only ones; women stray, too. Maybe it's a one-time thing, maybe they don't feel like they're getting any attention and somebody gives them attention. Human beings are complex. We're formed and informed by so many elements: our social environments; our religious or cultural upbringings; the relationships we grew up witnessing. I don't believe there's a 'one-size-fits-all'-type of relationship for all of us. But I do believe that people are resilient, and if somebody does leave somebody else, there's pain and anger and chaos, but with the passage of time, we grieve, recover, and then move on. We remember that life is worth living and there's much more to life than just your relationship status.

That said, I'm mainly only familiar with America—strictly middle-age, middle-class, white society—and I don't know as much about younger or older generations, or how other ethnicities do it.

The Influence of Technology on Marriage

The internet has changed the game, and not just for dating, but marriage, too. For the first time, people with 'unpopular' or 'underground' opinions on how things should be done can find whole online communities that think and feel just like them, and they're less completely isolated and cut off from the rest of the world and from each other. They're looking around and saying, "You know, this makes sense. Why can't our [government, religion, culture] be more accommodating for this or that?" And the next thing you know, we have same-sex marriage, plural marriages, kids being raised communally instead of just by their biological parents. The heteronormative nuclear family is a relatively recent concept compared to some of these more ancient traditions—traditions that along the way became prohibited by a culture or a religion that said, "That's not right." Now people are coming around and saying, "Actually, some of this stuff makes sense; let's go back to that. Let's let the tribe raise the kids."

In Austin, I've seen families form unofficial groups of four or five or ten for the purposes of duty-sharing. They still all keep their own houses and incomes, sleep in their own beds, but they pitch in around child-rearing, forming carpools or other 'taskforces' that allow the parents to take turns doing a little less work. The parents obviously benefit and I think the kids like it, too, this group upbringing. When they get older, and don't need their parents as much, then they form their own groups and gangs, and the internet makes it easier to partition those subgroups as well.

Once the parents aren't 'needed' as parents anymore, then they are again partners in a relationship. What does that look like now that the kid's left? *Do we want to be in this partnership, or have my interests changed? Could my life be better over here or there?* The fastest-growing demographic of divorces are late-in-life divorces, so-called 'gray divorces.'[1] One partner says: "I don't want to spend the rest of my golden years with you, good bye." It's even more common for the other partner to say, "Yeah, okay, me too," or to genuinely wish for their spouse more happiness and thus they part on good terms. It does seem skewed toward more women dumping their husbands late in life than men dumping their wives. They think, *Hey, I'm only 58 and I don't want 30 more years of this guy. I've done a lot of work for him and for our family, and now I want to do stuff for myself, and be independent and have my own freedom—or at least not have to answer to so many of my husband's expectations.* My mom divorced my dad late in life for this reason.[2]

Technology has also made it easier to 'screen' people for certain deal-breakers. If I'd met Christa on-

---

1 http://www.pewresearch.org/fact-tank/2017/03/09/led-by-baby-boomers-divorce-rates-climb-for-americas-50-population/

2 About seven years after their divorce, my dad realized that he was getting older, and had a lot of health issues, and he was scared of being alone. He remarried because he wanted some companionship. The sad thing was, his second wife had dementia, and within two years she'd deteriorated so much that she couldn't even be there, cognitively-speaking, for him in the way he'd wanted. Dad became more and more of her caregiver, which was a cruel trick of karma, because he'd wanted a free caregiver. As a result, he became very resentful. He coped by reaching out to a friend—in this case, another elderly, lonely female—and their friendship evolved into an intimate relationship that they hid for four or five years. The tremendous guilt and shame ate him alive, but for my siblings and I, who recognized what was going on, it made our father seem very human. Humans are social animals; we all crave connection. We would have supported him, but Dad never wanted to talk about it, because it didn't fit the very narrow definition of American marriage.

line and her internet dating profile had said, "I don't want to have kids ever," I probably wouldn't have messaged her. Same thing if she'd written "I want more than four kids." Or if she'd come from a different religious background, or we'd had conflicting personal philosophies ... generally, these are higher-level considerations that you get around to after you've known a person for a while, and decided whether or not you like them as a person. But when they're out in the open, front and center, before you've even said hello or seen their smile—I mean, yeah, you might miss out on meeting your soulmate because of something they wrote for the world to see that may or may not even be true.

Christa and I dated for three or four years before we got married, and then waited as many years again before having Drake. It was green lights all the way through: no surprises that made me question my choice of a mate. The trick is finding someone with whom, when the hormones, the pheromones, and the romance wears off, you can work together as partners.

FOMO, or the Fear of Missing Out, is a relatively new phenomenon fueled by dating apps that make it super easy to constantly be meeting new people. We wonder, *Is there something better? Is there a hotter person? A funnier person? Is there a wealthier person? Is there ...*

Unfortunately, this search for the ever-more-perfect partner is at ever-more-daunting odds with the fact that what people need to complete themselves, they can only find in themselves—never externally; never through a partner (or more money, or a medal, or a title).

Parenting and Marriage

I enjoyed having a brother when I was growing up. We were only two years apart, and pretty close, and I always thought that having a kid would be like having another little brother to play with. So I figured I would get married along the way and probably have one or two kids, and that's what happened. I met Christa in the mid-1990s and we had our son, Drake, three years later.

We never talked about having more kids, or a large number of kids, or adopting any kids. It just felt like life was unfolding as it was meant to. Plus, since my parents did get divorced late in life, I knew there was the possibility that marriage might not last forever—but was at least for as long as the kids were around and in the house, and we didn't need any more munchkins messing up the scene. In elementary and middle school, children of divorce were the minority. That most of our parents were still together then didn't mean that they were all really, really happy, but they stayed married. That's how it worked.

When my son was little, 'parenting' meant making sure he was safe, and teaching him, and exploring with him, and encouraging him to try some new things because he was a slow-to-warm kid. Now that he's a young adult, my parenting role is less direct. I provide advice and wisdom if he wants to ask me about things, but otherwise I try to keep my mouth shut because he's a smart kid and he needs to learn his own way of doing things. Sometimes I'll give him some technical information based on my own mistakes or experiences so that he doesn't fall into the same holes I did, like when it comes to renting a car or making a major purchase, because we all do some things for the first time ever. Other times, I'll just give him my two cents in a gentle way.

Drake would say that being an only child never caused him to miss out on anything. Really, he had the best of all worlds: no siblings with whom to have to divide his parents' love and attention, and plenty of friends to hang out with at school and on the weekends.

If and when Drake enters a serious relationship—so serious that they have a kid—I'll probably enjoy being a grandparent. People say it's all the fun of raising kids without the hassle, and that sounds great. Either way, it's not going to be the thing I center my life around. I grew up in a typical suburban household where we had our own place and there weren't multiple generations living with us. My siblings I didn't do many sleepover parties; it was very much each family to his own. With Drake, we got to know a few of his classmates' families, and there were a lot more sleepovers. Maybe people trust each other more today? At any rate, I hope we'd get to keep my son's kid(s) for a sleepover now and then.

Was I looking for particular 'mothering' traits in Christa when we married? Not really. I just wanted somebody who I would value as a partner, who seemed kind and conscientious and not selfish or self-centered. Kids demand a lot of attention, and Christa and I naturally fell into traditional gender roles when he was born. She stayed at home and did most of the domestic chores during the week. I worked full-time, but tried to spend more time with Drake on the weekends to give her a break. To this day, Christa does more of the cooking, cleaning, and shopping, and I handle our finances.

I don't know how much of it's biology, and how much is our culture saying "When we pair off, she's mine and I'm hers, and nobody should be messing up our strong pair bond." The biological imperative probably comes from knowing who the father is. *Who's responsible for raising this kid?* But the whole weird idea of scarcity in love and affection—that's definitely societal. It appeared as the nuclear family replaced the tribe: the notion that when you find love, you have to grab it and can't risk letting anyone else in, or you'll lose it and go back to being alone. That's a scarcity mindset, and it comes from having only two partners to raise a kid instead of a tribe.

I'm not convinced that the nuclear family model is the easiest or best way to raise kids, but at least I understand it. It goes back to the rugged American/Western European individualism of "Every man for himself" and "I'm not sharing" and "We're trying to get ahead and do better than you." Competition rather than cooperation.

Extramarital Relationships—or On Being "Monogamish"

Most marriage contracts restrict intimacy to two people: the man and wife, or the two husbands, or the two wives. But seemingly just as many married people have (either overtly or covertly) various levels of emotional, spiritual, or even physical relationships outside the marriage relationship. To what degree it's allowed or encouraged depends of course on the specific relationship.

Maybe a wife has regular 'girls weekends' with

her friends, or a husband takes hunting or fishing trips with his buddies. A businessman or woman goes out of town for a conference; they get drunk at the bar; there's a one-night stand. Some spouses take separate vacations and what happens in Vegas stays in Vegas. There's a Don't Ask, Don't Tell policy—an understood wink and a nod. Still other couples are more explicit about sharing information. They acknowledge that, "Hey, over time, I can't meet or be everything you need; so let's arrange something."

Those partners who feel they don't fit the mold of what a traditional marriage should be sometimes struggle to overcome the shame and the stigma. One partner might broach the topic of an open relationship, or being monogamish, only to be met with horror from their spouse. Then s/he cheats. Or, the partner feels so ashamed that s/he never brings it up—and then still cheats. Once the spouse finds out (as they invariably do), now it's not just the act of cheating, but the fact that their husband or wife lied. *How much time and energy are you diverting away from me and toward the other person?* they want to know. There's a sense of betrayal and loss. A *What do you mean I'm not everything to you? I was when we first met. What changed?*

What changed is that one or both partners discovered a need that they believed could only be met by someone else. And however you feel about that, I think it's better to have open and honest communication.

For example, I belong to several personal growth groups for men. Attending those groups satisfies some of my unmet emotional needs. Similarly, I have a few very intimate spiritual connections with both men and women other than my wife. Christa knows, and what's more, she supports it. She actually thinks it's good and healthy to diversify, to have friends and find support beyond our marriage relationship, and so she has groups that she attends, too. They're a big part of her life, and I'm not part of it, and she doesn't expect me to be.

Where it gets touchier is the extramarital physical relationships. For professional swingers who have sex all the time, no strings attached, maybe it really is just a roll in the hay; but for me, sex has always required emotional intimacy and a spiritual connection. It's never 'just' sex. A one-night stand therefore doesn't much appeal to me. So Christa and I have weekends.

A few weekends a year, we go our separate ways and each meet up with a special friend who each of us has known for a long time. She and I don't talk about it in detail, but the understanding is mutual and it works for us.

I've heard other people call it a 'free pass'—where the husband or the wife (or both) get a mister or a mistress on the side. People get tired of eating the same menu items at the same restaurant. It's usually just for fun, to live a 'fantasy lifestyle' for an evening or a weekend, with no kind of huge emotional disruption in anyone's life.

Christa was actually a mistress to one of her professors during grad school, and that's how she described it: like a fairytale. The man was married, but a genius academic, very well known in his field, and he was bored at home. Once or twice a month, he'd take Christa to dinner and dancing, and the evening almost always culminated in sex at her apartment, but he never spent the night and always went back home to his wife. When I asked Christa what she got out of the arrangement, she said, “He was a brilliant man, and I enjoyed talking research with him. Plus I got to dress up and be taken out, and even though the promise of sex was understood, he was a nice guy and patient, and not after me just for the one thing.”

For Christa, who grew up poor, to be treated so lavishly, and given designer dresses to wear to the ballet, it probably was a dream come true. After about a year and a half, though, she realized the affair wasn't going any place, and it dissolved. She didn't fall in love with him; she admired him. He was a teacher, a mentor, a coach—maybe even a father figure. Plus, being older, he approached the physical parts of their relationship differently than say, your typical college frat boy, and she valued the intention and sensuality he introduced to her life. His wife must have known something was up—he wasn't getting home until one or two in the morning—but she looked the other way. She (rightly) figured Christa wasn't the first and wouldn't be the last.

I guess what I'm trying to say is that I'm not anti-monogamy, and nor do I recommend being “monogamish.” But if you're going to try it, I do think couples need to be brave enough to have open conversations about what their needs are, or they risk destroying the relationship. It requires a lot of trust, a lot of communication, and its chances for success depend heavily on the strength of the relationship to begin with. The couples that do the best with ‘free passes,’ or semi-open relationships, are the ones where the partners do have a deep connection. They really, really, do love each other and either don't have a lot of fears that the other is going to wander off, or else they know that things change and there's always that possibility, but if you try to put a lid on it from the very beginning, then it's only going to lead to cheating and lies.

Everyone has to find what works for them. I just think we should all be free to choose. In general, I see less coercion and repression these days the world over, and that's a good thing. We all deserve to be happy, and what makes one person happy won't be and shouldn't be what makes someone else happy.

The Future of Marriage

Austin is a fairly liberal and accepting town compared to the rest of Texas. You'll find some pretty intelligent people here who have some pretty interesting and intelligent relationships that work. Whether it's open marriage, polyamory, traditional partners who swing, or who are having short-term or long-term affairs, it all comes down to the same concern: can you do it without causing too much hassle for yourselves, for the family, for the kids? And still have the lifestyle you want? One where nobody feels like they're being used or getting hurt?

By and large there still exists the normal funnel, which sweeps most people into heteronormative, traditional marriages that they may never question. But at least our ideas and options are becoming a bit more rational and flexible in general, to better match what serves humankind and human relationships beyond strictly legal values. Does it upset the Texan fundamentalists? Hell yeah, because they see changing values and they don't like it and it's uncomfortable. But it shouldn't concern anyone other than the two, or three, or four consenting adults, and the kids if there are any. That's the most important consideration I've taken away from mediating divorces: making sure that the kid reaches 15, 16, 17 psychologically intact and gets launched into adulthood okay.

So long as the kid has food and shelter and education and love, it doesn't matter how they get to adulthood. Single parents can raise kids successfully, though having a partner makes it easier. Having more partners, or a whole community, is probably even better. Living in a society that's friendly to child-rearing—that offers flexible work hours and paid maternity and paternity leave—is best of all.

So, does marriage serve a function? Yes: it's one expression of love, and it has certain legal benefits. Will it have a place in future societies? Of course—but it likely won't look the way it does today, or did ten years ago, because people change and societies change and it is the prerogative of the people to create and recreate a society that serves their highest good.

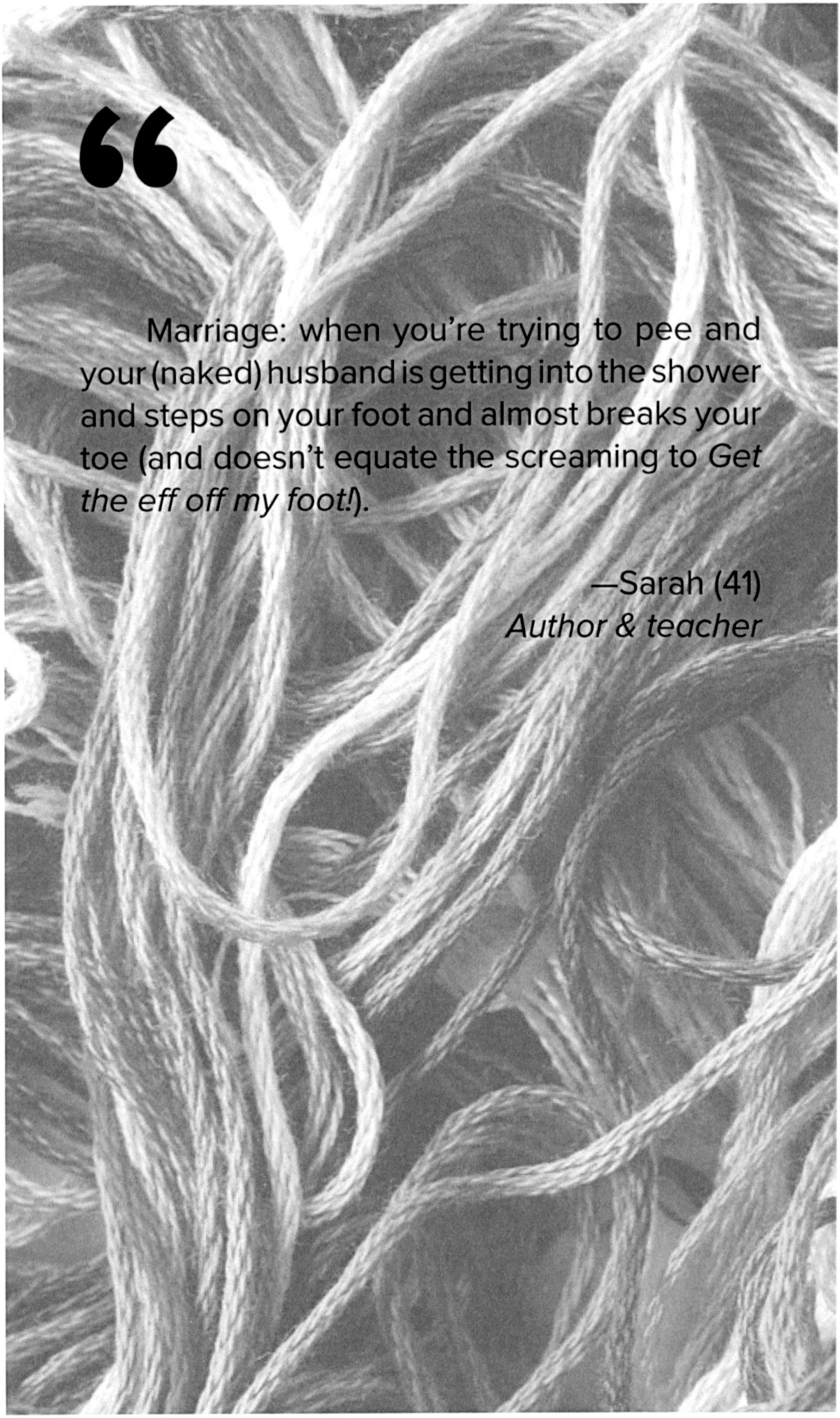

Marriage: when you're trying to pee and your (naked) husband is getting into the shower and steps on your foot and almost breaks your toe (and doesn't equate the screaming to *Get the eff off my foot!*).

—Sarah (41)
Author & teacher

JULIE & PRABIN

[Julie (31) and Prabin (36) met when Julie's father signed her up for IndianMatrimony.com, an online matchmaking site for single people of Indian descent. This 'new alternative' to arranged marriage takes concepts like love and attraction into account, but parents retain some power over determining their adult children's future spouses. Julie works as a purchaser for a home-builder in Austin; Prabin must wait for his American citizenship to process before finding work.]

2016

Julie: Prabin and I have been legally married for one whole day. He arrived in the United States (from India) just last week. It's his first time in the country, and everything is new and different. I was raised in Missouri, but he grew up in Kerala, and then worked abroad for a time in Norway, so his understanding of the United States was previously limited to movies, books, the news, and what I told him over the many hours we spent Skyping when we were first getting to know each other.

He's actually probably adjusting to life here better than me. I've never lived with a significant other before, so there's a lot of figuring out how to make my schedule accommodate him and his needs. For example, I normally knock out a trip to the grocery store in like 15 minutes. I know what I need and I go in and get it. But when Prabin went with me to the store, we spent an hour just wandering up and down the aisles, taking in all the new sights, from people to products.

This is only Weekend #2 with him, but so far I'm getting much less done on the weekends than I would have by myself. If we get to the grocery store, and fit in a workout before cooking dinner together, then it's a good day. I know we'll get more efficient as we get our systems down. Maybe like a divide-and-conquer, with one person going to the grocery store and the other person taking care of something else, but right now we're just trying to get our bearings.

Our wedding yesterday was pretty last-minute. We'd planned to do a simple courthouse ceremony in the middle of last week, but when we went to get our marriage license we found out we had to wait 72 hours after obtaining the license to actually say "I do." I don't know why that rule is in place; maybe so people don't make hasty decisions? In Texas, you don't need any witnesses. The judge just signs your certificate, and then you return it to the Travis county office and they record it.

Prabin started calling the list of available judges that the county had given us, and found one who said he'd be willing to marry us in our neighborhood park. So we did it yesterday! The judge seemed really nice, but it was an unfortunately cold day and not many of our friends were able to attend. It's okay though, because we're planning a more formal ceremony for next summer. This event was just to get the legal part out of the way, since we still have a few more steps to take to get Prabin's green card.

The whole ceremony lasted ten minutes max. We requested generic, nondenominational vows—again, because we will be writing our own vows next summer. He and I agree that unless you've chosen a person to write your vows for you who knows you very well, you should write them yourself. How could you let someone else dictate the premises of what you're promising each other? After speaking aloud our generic vows, we went for brunch at L'oca d'Oro and had an otherwise very relaxing afternoon.

Probably our story sounds weird to people outside the Indian culture. I'm half-Indian, the daughter of an Irish Catholic mother and a Hindu father, so I wasn't necessarily raised with traditional Indian values. As I approached age 30, my father started to worry that the marriage pool was narrowing. He was very concerned about seeing me 'settled down,' so he signed me up on the Indian matrimony site. He created a profile for me, then gave me a chance to review it and add a little more personal flavor. I kind of let it sit on the back burner for a while, preoccupied with my 'real' life here in Austin.

The longer I let it go, the more my dad got into it. He started browsing profiles of potential matches, and sending me ID numbers (every profile gets assigned an ID number) to check out. At one point he asked, "Have you seen the Norway guy?" I had not, so I reached out to this guy—who was Prabin—and we started messaging through the site. Soon we moved to email, and from there to WhatsApp, and within a week we had our first phone call. On that call, I realized we had a lot in common. We seemed to share a big-picture perspective, having many of the same priorities and goals. Pretty quickly we decided we wanted to meet, aware that sometimes things pan out differently in person. We didn't want to get too far into it without making sure we had the physical chemistry.

Prabin: The timing was everything for me. In 2014, I graduated university and knew I had a small window to pursue personal goals before becoming consumed by my career. After a bit of soul-searching, I decided that one of those goals was to meet and marry a life partner. Several friends had successfully used Indian-Matrimony.com, and were very happy with the wives their parents had found for them through the site, so I tried it out. I created my own profile; my family didn't know anything about it. I worried that they'd choose the wrong person—that my parents or immediate relatives would select a partner who was way different from the one I would choose for myself. I had the profile for about a year, and exchanged a few messages here and there with women who showed great promise, only to find out somewhere down the line that we wanted different things and it just didn't feel right.

Then, after three and half years living abroad, I moved back to India. I reconnected with my family and my cousin tried to set me up with her friend's niece. I went as far as meeting her. We got coffee and chatted, and she was really nice, but she wasn't my kind of girl. She didn't like traveling or any of the things I liked. So I said, "I'm done with this whole dating thing and I'm taking a break and moving back to Norway and focusing on my work." That's when I got Julie's message: in November 2015.

Several things stood out to me about her profile. I wanted somebody with a lot of Indian-ness, but who is also independent, had lived abroad, etc. Her profile said she liked traveling and hiking, and that she lived in Austin, Texas but had been to India and many other countries besides. Our first call went off on the right note. In the first ten minutes we were talking about where we wanted to travel next and how that's all we wanted to do, and I shared my philosophy of a life that fit in a backpack. It was just very easy. We were texting; there was compatibility from the beginning. So that's how it started.

Julie: Prabin's profile stood out because it seemed really well-rounded. The other profiles focused more on professional development: people just boasting about what they've accomplished. I wanted someone who had a lot of varied interests and hobbies—a dynamic person—because there's more to life than your career, especially at some points in your life.

Marrying within the Indian culture was not originally important to me. I could see the benefits of doing so: for example, Indians value education and family life highly. But I felt like as long as the commitment was there, it didn't matter what culture he came from. Unfortunately, it's harder to screen for 'commitment level' on sites like Match.com, whereas IndianMatrimony.com has the word 'matrimony' built right into the name. We're obviously all there for the same reason.

If you ask me, the first Skype call was slightly awkward. Or maybe 'sterile' is the right word. I was pretty nervous, and kept the conversation congenial. I remember talking about our favorite authors. Prabin later told me that he was 'playing it safe,' too—sticking to 'diplomatic' topics because he didn't hold out much hope after several failed experiences with other women on the site. There wasn't exactly a warm connection to begin with.

Prabin: But then we Skyped every day for two weeks, and for as long as four or five hours on Sundays. At which point I suggested we meet in person. My litmus test was, *If I can travel with a complete stranger for a week, and by the end of the trip we don't want to kill each other—then that's a good sign.* It was important to me that Julie and I build our fledgling relationship on something real, not just cyber-chatting.

Julie already had plans to travel to Nicaragua with friends in December, so we postponed meeting until January. Somewhere in Europe felt like the natural 'halfway point' for us to meet, but of course January is wintertime over there, meaning it had to be the Mediterranean. We each did some research and mutually chose Sicily. Not only was it warmer, but I'm a big *Godfather* fan.

Those two months felt like a long time to wait.

Come January, I flew from Norway to Berlin to Rome, then took a bus from the airport to the cafe at which we'd arranged to meet. Julie's flight was delayed by half an hour, and I kept checking my phone, wondering where she was and if I was being stood up. I even thought she might have reached the cafe, taken one look at me, and ran off! But I kept sitting there with my backpack and my camera, ready to capture the moment should she appear.

Finally she walked in, and I managed to get a shot of her and her luggage. It took us a couple hours (and a couple glasses of wine) after that to feel comfortable with one another. She'd never traveled for a week with a stranger before, and I'm a backpacker, so solo travel is my norm. By the end of the first evening, we'd effectively broken the ice.

Julie: That was a really long day. We met around 10:00 or 11:00 in the morning, had lunch, and then went back to the airport to catch a flight to Palermo, Sicily that evening.

The first thing I had to do was call my dad, of course. He was supportive of the trip, but wanted to make sure that everything was okay and I felt good about being with Prabin. There is some risk inherent in making a trip like that ... but if you don't take the risk, you won't ever know.

Prabin: Julie is really easy to be around. We didn't have a single fight or issue come up the whole week. She did have to tell me to slow down one time, when I kind of got stuck in my head and lapsed into my own way of doing things, forgetting that she was there. I think I was rushing ahead to see something, and she stopped me and asked, "Prabin, what are you doing? This is my vacation time. This is my chill time. Have you seen *The Amazing Race*?" she joked.

I realized I had to move at her pace. "Okay," I conceded, "go ahead. I'll follow you."

For the most part, we wanted to do the same things anyway. Find a hole-in-the-wall place for dinner, eat good food, drink good wine, and walk around aimlessly, soaking it all up.

My family still didn't know anything about Julie at this point. They didn't even know that I was 'talking' to a girl. They rarely knew what part of the world I was in at any given time. I guess I didn't tell them about Julie because I didn't want to jinx it. I was getting older, and they were giving up hope that I would ever get married. "This guy," they'd say, shaking their heads. "We don't know how to deal with him, so let him do what he feels like." Sometimes I'd send them pics from Italy, Lithuania, Germany—wherever my travels took me.

On the second to last day of our trip, we were back in Rome and the thought crossed my mind to propose. Julie and I had met; she had clearly passed the litmus test. What now? Should I wait until the next trip, in 3-4 months' time, or should I just ask her already? No one was there with me to talk it through, and it was difficult to think clearly, in each other's faces 24/7.

I don't know how Julie felt. She might have wanted to wait longer, but I had to try. So on our last night in Rome, we're in the hotel room talking and I'm like, "Let's do it." I got down on one knee and proposed to her.

That hotel room wasn't the most romantic place, but now we just tell people that we got engaged in Rome, and they immediately picture the Basilica or something like that. It's the picture they get in their heads, even though the reality was totally different.

Julie: I was completely shocked. I wasn't expecting him to do that at all. But saying yes came naturally. Prabin is everything I'd been looking for in a partner—that much became clear while we were traveling. He's not lacking in any areas. He has a curiosity for life; he's interested in art museums and photography; he can appreciate creativity; and he's just a really good traveler. I saw him interact with the local people and try to genuinely get to know the culture. We spent one whole afternoon watching a group of elderly people at a cafe. They were having a great time and we had so much fun observing them. Prabin enjoys the simple things in life, and I felt present and able to just kick back and be with him.

He's also a really good cook, and I like his sense

of humor.

Prabin: So she called her dad, and I think he was a little shocked, too, like *Isn't it a bit soon?* He'd wanted to meet me first. But Julie and I were trying to make things work across three continents, and the practical part of me knew that we needed to cut down the distance, and soon. After she said "yes" to the whole marriage thing, I said, "It doesn't make sense for you to move to Norway, because then we'll both be unstable, so I'll come to you." I quit my job, went home to India, and started the lengthy immigration process. It took nearly 8 months.

The process isn't difficult per se, but it is difficult to be patient with procedure. For the past five years, I'd been filing the paperwork to renew my working visa annually, so I guess I'm used to it. Still, I'd get frustrated sometimes and vent to Julie, but she'd just say, "It's okay, we'll get there." Luckily things went as smoothly as they could, and I got the green light in November.

I finally told my family about Julie on the journey back to Oslo from Rome. I texted them from a Copenhagen bus in the middle of the night: "Hey, I just got engaged." They were like, "Don't be ridiculous, Prabin. Marriage is not a joke. We know you're fooling us." Because I could tell they didn't believe me, I sent them photos from our trip then called my parents over wifi on WhatsApp.

"No, this is really happening," I said. "I'll give you more details later, but right now I'm traveling back to Norway."

They still didn't believe it, and it took them some time to understand it. When I got back to Oslo I gave my parents and my brother the whole story. On the one hand, they were very happy for me—but cautiously so. Their skeptical natures had them convinced that I was trying to pull off some elaborate prank. I don't think those fears rested until Julie and her dad came to Kochi.

Julie: That was in July. It was Prabin's first time meeting my dad, and my first time meeting Prabin's family. I had talked to his parents on the phone, and I'd met his cousins who live in New York and Atlanta (they flew to Austin to say hello), but the Kochi trip was really the first interaction that counted. I felt some pressure to make a good impression, but I also tried to enjoy being back in India. It'd been about three years since my last visit. I used to go more often, back when my grandmother was still alive.

Unfortunately, my dad's family speaks Tamil (I can understand more Tamil than I can speak) and Prabin's family speaks a completely different dialect called Malayalam, so my limited language skills weren't of much use. While most of Prabin's family also speaks English, they're shy about doing so, and some of them don't at all. Those who do know English don't use it very often, meaning the conversation was a little forced, a little more halting and superficial than I would have liked. Prabin is now teaching me a few words in Malayalam every day, and he's given me his old textbooks to work through. I hope I become more proficient in the language soon.

Prabin: The conversation may have been hard, but everyone really liked Julie anyway. They accepted her into the family immediately, saying she resembles my mom in a lot of good ways.

I'm not sure the same can be said of me and Julie's father. He landed in India a few hours before she did, so I went to pick him up from the airport and we had some time to kill together without her. It's always awkward meeting the father of the girl you're dating, but I tried to put on a good show. I felt like I had to break the ice, so I said some nice things about his daughter and tried to calm his fears about our relationship. Somewhere he'd gotten the impression that I'm not a very serious guy, which was working against me. My impression of Julie's dad is that he's pretty chill, and really listens to what people say. He takes his time responding; he's a thoughtful dude.

It was his idea to have a little engagement party in India, since we won't be getting married in-country. About 40 people came—mostly relatives of Julie's dad who live in India, and a couple of my friends and my brother.

Julie: After the India trip, Prabin and I returned to our respective countries and weren't sure when we would see each other again. Everything depended on how fast the paperwork was processed. He had to interview at the Indian embassy, and pass an American test to be approved.

Those months were harder than any we'd gone through yet. It's hard to live your separate lives and not share experiences firsthand. Even if you talk for a couple hours every day, you can still only share the highlights. It becomes hard to keep the momentum going, and remember that you're working toward something bigger.

It didn't help that every month, Prabin would take

off into the jungle to go hiking (he wasn't working at this time, having quit his job in Norway and reluctant to start something new in India when his American visa could come through at any moment), and I wouldn't hear from him for a week. He'd be trekking through remote areas without internet, so it was radio silence. Every time he got back in contact with me, I felt relief mixed with an irritation that usually resulted in a fight. I thought about making another trip to India, and would have if the visa hadn't come through when it did.

Prabin landed at JFK on Thanksgiving Day. No problems with immigration. I flew up there to meet him, and we spent a couple days playing tourists in New York City, and a couple more with his family in Jersey. And now it's been a week and a day since Prabin moved in with me in Austin!

Prabin: It was an eighteen-hour flight from Kerala to New York. I caught a cab from the airport, from which I got my first taste of the United States. I was surprised, first of all, by the size of everything—from the roads to the bridges. I didn't expect it to be so big and massive in scale. I've been to Dubai, and Dubai is pretty big, but it's nothing compared to New York City.

The third week of November there was reasonably warm. The trees were still turning and I thought everything was very beautiful. Compared to Europeans, I find Americans to be open and friendly, making my adjustment that much easier. I'm unfamiliar with the topography here, and I think U. S. public transit sucks, but other than that everything seems to be all right. I'm not a traveler; I'm legal. I live here now, so I'm trying to understand it all ... which means I bombard Julie with a lot of probably very annoying questions.

She's been patient though.

In Norway, I was running a digital marketing firm and worked as a freelance consultant. I have three master's degrees, so I'm not too worried about finding work in Texas, and I'm actually thankful to have a mandatory break from work during my probation period here. I want to learn to drive, and do some writing, and maybe make some art. I'm used to working 'round the clock and always being on the move. Essentially, I'm learning to relax for the first time. Landing around the holidays was lucky, because everyone's in vacation mode and moving a bit more slowly right now anyway.

Also, it's 'real life' now. Before, we were traveling together and doing all the fun stuff. Now we're planning our days, our weeks, our lives. It's the longest we've been in the same place together.

Julie: Our next task will be to start wedding planning—as in, the actual formal ceremony. It won't be a religious wedding. Prabin's Hindu and I'm Catholic, but he only goes to temple sometimes and I never go to church. It will be more about the party. Less Big Fat Indian Wedding and more a function for our extended families to meet each other.

Prabin: The wedding next summer will be the fourth time that we exchange rings. When I first proposed in Rome, I knew I had to get her something symbolic before she went back, so I bought a one-Euro ring from a church and put it on her finger, promising her a proper one later. We then had rings made for each other to exchange in India, in front of her dad and my family. The third time was yesterday for the judge.

To me, the ring is a reminder and reinforcement

that we are married. It symbolizes that I'm not a single vagabond anymore; I have responsibilities and I've made a commitment and I trust in my relationship. Whenever I see it or feel it, it's just like, *Oh, I'm married.* The band is my bond.

Julie: I feel similarly. It's a reminder of our connection and commitment to each other.

What's funny though is that I think marriage means something different to everyone. You see one example by watching your parents; you get a second perspective in movies, or by watching people in the street; and then other couples are always trying to give you advice. But the terms of the agreement look different for everybody. Some couples want more space and to only see each other on the weekends. Some want to do everything together.

I just try to remember that there will always be ups and downs, and that at the end of the day, I enjoy life more when I'm sharing it with someone else. It's nice to share in the bad times and the good. Having gone through those experiences together adds to your marriage and makes it more solid. We also waited to get married a bit later in life, so we had clear-cut ideas of what we wanted.

Prabin: Julie and I are more well-rounded, more mature, than either set of our parents were when they got married. Both unions were love marriages, but they were young and didn't really know what they were getting into. People didn't 'date' as much back then.

The analogy I draw is to a travel experience. When you visit a place, the experience is your own, and while you can come back and show your friends pictures, they don't really get it. They're like, "Wow, that's cool," but they can't ever share the experience just by looking at snapshots of it.

Marriage is the same. What other people see, and what really happens between two people, are very different things. I could describe every second of day-to-day living with Julie, and you still won't feel what we feel.

Like many couples, Julie and I communicate best nonverbally. We haven't told each other that we love each other yet. I'm not very vocal to begin with, plus I take my time with things.

Julie: I think both marriage and love will look different at different stages. The thing that Prabin and I have created between us ... it's living, it's breathing, and it changes. I want to be open to that rather than having too many expectations. You have to have patience with one another, and genuinely want the best for your partner. You don't have to know all the answers; you just have to ride the wave.

I don't believe in soul mates. Love isn't pre-destined; it's work. And maybe one person is only 'right' for you during a certain part of your life, and someone else is right later. But I believe marriage is something you enter, more or less, for life. There are only a few reasons I would exit a marriage.

Prabin: I don't believe in soul mates, either. But I do believe in karma, and I believe that when something is bound to happen, the universe conspires to help nudge it along. Somewhere along the way, a lot of coincidences fell into place to lead Julie and me to this moment.

Julie: We will have to give each other a lot of grace during this initial adjustment period, and acknowledge that we've each been living alone for some time. It will take some time to sync our rhythms. We've only started dusting the surface, and now we're going to the core of who we are. That takes a bit of unraveling. Who knows what will happen?

2017

Julie: I know it's probably a cliche; everyone says your wedding day is a blur and it just flies by, but it does. You spend all your time planning it, and then the day of—all those little details you obsessed over? You don't even notice those details because you're so busy. You have to ask the guests, "Hey, how was this? How was that?" Like you weren't even present at your own wedding.

But then afterward, you get to look through all the photos of your family and close friends being together in one place, and it's really touching to see how happy everyone looks for you. Prabin's dad and best friend flew in from India. His cousin came from Singapore. One of my friends from Amsterdam came. The rest of the guests represented nine different states.

I thought I'd have more time to sit and chat with individual groups of people. No one told me that on your wedding day, everyone comes up to you and says "Congratulations!" and you say "Thanks!" and that's about it. We even had an Indian-themed party the night before (where everyone wore *saris*) so that we would have time to catch up on each other's lives, but it didn't really happen. And we only had 70 guests! I can't imagine what it would have been like with more.

Prabin & Julie

We decided to have the wedding at a remote ranch forty minutes outside of Denver. There were cabins on the property, so people could stay at the venue. It was about 9,000 feet up, just kind of nestled in the mountains. No one had cell service, so we took the opportunity to relax and bond with nature. In that intimate setting, our families really got to know each other.

Prabin: Wedding planning and the wedding itself were definitely the first tests of marriage. It was stressful working within so many constraints, and on a budget. Most of our arrangements had to be made over the phone. Trying to coordinate that many people was insane. Luckily, a few months before the wedding we were able to fly to Colorado and see the ranch firsthand. I found the venue and designed the invitations; after that, I threw my hands up and Julie did the rest.

Julie: It wasn't that bad. The biggest thing in the beginning is finding and booking a venue. Once you have that, you can kinda coast for a while, until maybe the last six weeks. Then stuff comes to a head.

The other big challenge was getting responses from vendors. I wanted to run through and confirm everything, but the mountain folk were a little more lax. Plus they do a lot of weddings in just a few months.

For something like a wedding, where you set out to do it just once (get married, that is), the day carries a lot of weight. You have certain expectations; you want it all to be 'just so.' But once you're in the thick of it, as time goes on, you just want to 'get on with the show' so to speak.

We got married the day before the Fourth of July,

which was a Monday this year. It worked out because most people had the holiday weekend off.

Prabin: The most stressful part was after the wedding. Before the wedding, you're stressed about how it will go. After the wedding, you just want to relax and put your feet up—but that's the time you have to meet everyone who flew in for the event and thank them all and entertain them all.

Julie: Another adjustment to being married is that now you have your spouse's family to think about. Most people start out with two families: their mom's side and their dad's side. Now you add in your new spouse's maternal and paternal relatives and it's like making the rounds at the holidays. You want to see everyone, and you want to keep it fair, but there's a lot of people to satisfy. We managed by inviting everyone to stick around Colorado for a few more days and hang out and go whitewater rafting. Since we didn't take a honeymoon, we're thinking about going to South America early next year—or whenever Prabin gets his green card. He still can't step out of the country.

Prabin: Nothing about our ceremony was very traditional. We had two people—family members—officiate the service. It was nondenominational. It lasted fifteen minutes. We wrote our vows to each other that morning, a bit hungover and slumped in chairs facing opposite directions.

The one symbolic gesture we included was the tying of the *tali*, the equivalent of a wedding ring in Indian culture. Typically, the groom puts this small charm on a gold chain around the bride's neck, and it symbolizes the sacred bond they're entering. An Indian woman won't remove the *tali* once it's placed. I gave Julie a gold leaf charm on a gold thread. She's not wearing it because we need to get a chain to replace the thread.

Julie: So our big wedding was four months ago now, Prabin's been in the country for over a year ... and we're still experiencing growing pains. I thought the rhythm of our lives might sync up more, but it's challenging. I get up at 6:30, even on the weekends. I like to go to the gym, go shopping, and have my day laid out before me. Prabin doesn't get up before 10:00 unless he has a cricket match, and he really comes alive in the evening, just as I'm ready to hit the bed. We try to compromise, especially on the weekends, but sometimes if I take it more chill in the mornings for him, then I get stressed when it's 2:00 and I haven't accomplished what I wanted to get done.

Being married is about figuring out how to merge two different people's very different priorities. Compromise is important, but so is protecting what's important to you. If something throws you off that much, it may make sense to hold your ground there and give ground somewhere else.

What helps is finding stuff we like to do together—whether that's running, or playing tennis, or cooking. Usually one person cooks and the other is on clean-up duty, but it's still an activity we share. We go to the farmer's market or the movies; we try new restaurants and check out breweries. I think it's important to keep 'dating' each other. When you go out of your living space and you have dinner, there's just a better quality of conversation. You say, "This is our time," and then give each other undivided attention.

Prabin: I'm a very social person, but ever since Julie and I started living together, I've become more of a homebody. It's easy to slip into that mode, that comfort zone. We're aware of it, and now that we know who we are as a unit, I think we'll start stepping out more socially again. It's nice to have that built-in person you can do things with on demand. I'm having to rebuild my social circle from scratch over here.

I also want to take advantage of our freedom while we can. After soccer yesterday, one of the guys on my team was saying how having kids changes everything. He told me to "enjoy the honeymoon phase," reminiscing about how he and his wife used to be able to go and do whatever, whenever. Julie and I are still green on that, so when we say, "Marriage is so much work," it's because it's fresh, and we're caught up in the transition from singles to couple. And then to add some kids to it? Wow.

Julie: We definitely want kids, but we also want to introduce them on a solid foundation. I doubt there will ever be a morning when I wake up and say, "I have marriage figured out now and now is the perfect time for kids." But hopefully, with a bit more time and money under our belts ... In the meantime, we're going to enjoy our autonomy and keep traveling as much as we can, before backpacking with an infant becomes a logistical nightmare. It'd also be nice to do some more traveling before Prabin gets a job. The two weeks of vacation time we get here in America aren't exactly conducive to trip-taking.

Two days before our wedding, we drove from

Austin to Denver, and camped at Trinidad in between. It was my first legit camping trip, and we were totally unprepared. We had a tent, but it was new and we were trying to put it up for the first time in the dark. The weather channel hadn't predicted the freezing hail, and I didn't even have a sweatshirt. In retrospect, it's pretty funny, but that's the beauty of relationships: having someone to show you new things that you weren't exposed to before, and who gives you the courage to try new things.

Prabin: No one from my family gave me any advice about marriage, and I wouldn't have listened anyway if they had. Julie and I, we're a work in progress. We just take it one day at a time. As long as we can get drunk once in a while, get out somewhere, travel for a few days—even if it's in the U.S.—that's okay for us. For me, at least.

Julie: I wish more people had tried to give me advice, especially people who have been at this whole thing longer. I don't have any living grandparents, but you know, people who have kids or who have been married a long time, the reassurance they could offer—like, "Don't worry about that, those things don't matter in the long run ... or it'll even out, you'll find your rhythm." I think that type of information is really helpful. I think it's lost a little bit.

While marriage is different for everyone (there's no such a thing as a "normal" marriage), in the end we're also all human; we have the same desires and needs, emotionally. Everyone's working through their own struggle. It's never going to just be perfect. You have to constantly be adapting to whatever's happening around you, and communicate with your mate, and be strong together as an internal unit to handle whatever external factors are shifting and changing.

Like Prabin said, there might as well be a huge "Under Construction" sign on our marriage. We're still figuring a lot out, but it challenges us to be better. My boss always says, "Marriage teaches you how selfish you are, and having kids teaches you patience"—or something like that. Marriage puts a magnifying glass on your positives and your negatives, so you're forced to reflect on yourself. In that sense, I think marriage makes you a better person, because you're able to recognize where you're lacking and try to improve on that. And where your strengths are as well. Ideally, you can share your strengths with each other and you both can become better people.

“

[*from* “Why You Will Marry the Wrong Person”]

We need to swap the Romantic view for a tragic (and at points comedic) awareness that every human will frustrate, anger, annoy, madden, and disappoint us—and we will (without any malice) do the same to them. There can be no end to our sense of emptiness and incompleteness. But none of this is unusual or grounds for divorce. Choosing whom to commit ourselves to is merely a case of identifying which particular variety of suffering we would most like to sacrifice ourselves for.

—Alain de Botton (47)
Philosopher

JADE & MIKEY

[Jade (33) is a production editor, letterpress printer, and adjunct professor in Boulder, Colorado. She has been in a committed relationship with her partner Mikey (37), who works for Avery Brewing Co., since 2003—but the couple has consciously decided never to marry.]

2016

Mikey grew up with one of my Evergreen College roommates, Crystal. We met when he came to visit her at the end of freshman year. For the first eight months that we knew each other, he lived in Seattle—about an hour from the Olympia campus. He soon started visiting more regularly, first under the guise of seeing Crystal, and then because he wanted to see me.

Eventually Mikey moved to Olympia. He wasn't happy in Seattle, and had more friends in the Olympia area. We 'hung out' for the next year or so, nothing serious, until by junior year I was ready to move off campus. He and I decided to rent a big house with some of our friends. That was sort of the 'All right, we're really doing this' moment.

Music and art were two of the things that drew us together initially. Music is still a big part of our relationship. He's a musician and I'm a music-lover; we connected over that instantly, and everything else seemed to come easily. I was a broke college student and he was pretty broke from moving, so rather than go to concerts, we threw a lot of house parties where everyone just chilled and listened to CDs. We're both very social people, and the house was open to everyone, so it fit us.

While I studied Creative Writing, Mikey found a job at a restaurant and tapped into the downtown bar scene. He got a few of his friends from middle school together and they started playing informal gigs. Eighteen years old, I couldn't go to most of his shows, but it gave me time to focus on schoolwork and him time to re-establish himself in a new city.

Right before I met Mikey, I was casually dating—having just broken up with another boyfriend and pretty averse at the time to the idea of relationships. I was young and didn't know what I wanted, except that I didn't want to be tied down in any way. One of the first things I ever said to Mikey, once we acknowledged that we were more than friends, was "Just so you know, I never want to get married or have babies." I just wasn't interested.

Ironically, my parents met when they were 16 and they've been happily married for more than 40 years. I consider them a super strong model for marriage, yet I've never really believed in it. It doesn't feel necessary to me, or like a priority. As I've gotten older, I've watched a lot of my friends marry. Some of them will admit that they felt this 'societal pressure'—that marriage was the accepted (and expected) 'next step,' and they married because they were 'supposed' to, not because they felt a real connection to the idea.

So I think you can have a fulfilling relationship without it ending in marriage, and I also like the small social protest aspect. Limiting the reach of religion and the government keeps my relationship on my terms, instead of societal terms. Luckily, all of our parents are completely supportive and we're all very close to one another. If something happened where one of us had to be hospitalized and didn't have spousal visiting rights, I can't imagine a family member standing in our way.

As far as kids, I've always known I didn't want them. Even as a child, when my friends wanted to play House and argued over who would be the mom, I'd say, "Okay, I'm going to be the older sister." Today I have two dogs, but I don't know if I consider myself their 'dog mom.' Mikey tells people that's how he knows I'm a keeper—because I don't want kids. He's so easygoing that he'd probably go along with whatever his partner wanted. Like, it if was really important to me, he'd bend, whereas I wouldn't. If he really wanted kids, I'd say, "You're going to have to find someone else, because that's not in my plan."

Mikey and I have been together 14 years now—almost half my life. In all that time, we've never had a commitment ceremony of any kind, though we've talked about throwing a party because who doesn't want to dress up and have a day that's all about you? When we first moved to Colorado, I looked into the requirements for common-law marriage, but it's something you have to apply for, very much like a marriage license. Maybe someday we will, but neither of us feels the need to make some public declaration of commitment. Which is why we don't wear rings, either: it's already clear that we're committed to each other.

To me, being in a relationship (whether romantic or platonic) is all about respect and kindness. Care and consideration. The more intimate the relationship, the more collaboration it demands. You have to be aware of the other person and their needs, as well as your needs and how you affect each other. Being in a relationship is not necessarily synonymous with being monogamous—that's something both parties need to very clearly discuss and be on the same page about.

Before Mikey and I declared our relationship "exclusive," there were some pretty fluid boundaries. We 'betrayed' each other more than once; feelings got hurt. But we worked through that, and for now, monogamy makes sense to us. Is it the only model for a successful relationship? I don't think so. Like gender or sexuality or anything else, what works for someone at one point might change down the road. You have to be open to that, and if the new thing works for both of you—great. If it doesn't, which is unfortunately sometimes the case, then you have to grateful for what was and happy that your partner is stepping into something more authentically them.

In our case, Mikey and I feel pretty sure we knew each other in a past life. Our connection was just too strong from the beginning for it to be any other way. We met so relatively early in our lives, too (this go-around on the planet, anyway), that I can't imagine being with anyone else. But that doesn't mean we're independently the only other person we've each ever been with, through time and space, or that we're the only two to have experienced this inter-life connection. All I know is that he's an important part of this experience, now. He's my match.

I mean, I'm pretty agnostic actually—but I think I need to believe in past lives, and reincarnation, just so I don't completely shut down. The idea that we get one chance and one chance only—and if it's horrible, that's all you get—is the most depressing notion ever. Also, Mikey is not the only person I've experienced that feeling with in this lifetime. There have been several other occasions in which I've met someone for the first time, only to feel like, *Oh, you again!* That feels a little too powerful and tangible to not have some basis in reality.

Neither of us is particularly spiritual and we're definitely not religious. I work for a press that publishes spiritual texts, so I'm probably more influenced by certain philosophies than Mikey is, but basically I just try to be a good person. I treat others the way I want to be treated and try to be the best version of myself that I can be. I hold Mikey to that same standard, reminding him what he's capable of—what he can be—and supporting his parallel journey of continual self-improvement.

Like any couple, we've had our share of challenges. After I graduated from Evergreen, we moved to Austin for two years and then to Boulder. About six months after moving to Austin, Mikey's mom died unexpectedly, and he didn't handle it well at all. He'd just started a new job at a bar that encouraged heavy staff drinking and partying as part of the culture. In his grief, Mikey fell head over heels down that rabbit hole to a really dark, unhealthy place. I wasn't doing so well in Texas, either, and suggested that we try for a fresh start in Colorado. "But," I told him, "the person you have become isn't allowed to come with me. He stays here."

Mikey quit drinking cold turkey—for a while. To this day, he doesn't drink hard alcohol, but his drinking continues to be an issue. All I can do is keep the lines of communication clear and open. I've made it known what my needs are; it's up to him to decide if he wants to meet them or not. We all have our crap that comes up: our different demons. His take the forms of drinking and depression; mine manifest as anxiety and health problems. It's impossible for your issues not to affect those closest to you, whether friends, family, or lovers.

We'd moved to Austin so Mikey could scope out the music scene. We moved to Boulder so I could start grad school at Naropa. It was a two-year program, and I never expected to be here longer than that, but this fall marks eight years. We rent a house together, and strive to keep everything equitable. Certain bills are in his name and certain bills are in mine. Our financial accounts are separate, but we track it all on a whiteboard. If the water bill runs high one month, he'll toss a few extra bucks my way. If he's done all the grocery shopping recently, I make sure to get the next trip. It's not as rigid as it sounds; we're both of the mindset that so long as we take care of ourselves and each other, everything will work out. Chores work the same way. There are parts of the house I tend to clean more because I use them more, like the kitchen. But we also like to find times to clean together.

It's a system that's taken many, many years to figure out. You have to troubleshoot the glitches over and over again. Now we know our partner's preferences, and equally, what drives them crazy. We also know how best to show each other we care about each other.

For example, I believe actions speak louder than words. I hate when Mikey apologizes to me. *I don't want apologies; just don't do it again*. I appreciate small gestures. We don't give each other birthday or

Christmas presents, so when he surprises me with a bouquet of orange sunflowers just because he knows that I love the color orange and that sunflowers are my favorite, or when he makes dinner for me after I've had a hard day at work, it's so much more meaningful than a cardboard box of chocolates on Valentine's Day. We don't even celebrate our anniversary for that reason. (By the way, since we're not married, we use the day we met as a benchmark—like, *All right, another year of hanging around together!*)

The kindness, and the awareness, and the consideration we show to one another—these are the things that matter. Mikey's my main man. My partner in crime. The stability and support that he lends my life has allowed me to accomplish more, personally and professionally, than I would have been able to on my own. We have each other's backs during difficult times, and we give love on a daily basis. It's important.

It helps that we have great families who are quite open, loving, and accepting. No family relationship is perfect—everyone has their tensions and issues and histories—but in general we all get along and tease each other only in good fun. Mikey has two younger brothers and I have an older sister. Ironically, her divorce got finalized last week. She was married for 17 years and had three kids with her husband. Mikey's middle brother is getting married next summer and Mikey will be the best man in the wedding. So, again, it's not like marriage is a foreign concept in our family—it's just not for us.

Occasionally someone will ask if our views on marriage have changed. Our families don't pressure us; they're just curious. I say "Nope" and nothing else and they don't push it. They're just happy that we're happy. They care that we have a healthy relationship and a good life together, no matter what that looks like. Right now we're talking about buying a house. We're trying to figure out if we want to do that, and if so, where. That's the biggest #relationshipgoal on the horizon.

Other than that, we're both vegetarians, we both have dreadlocks, and we love collecting records and eating good food. We maintain our independence, but there's space for collaboration, too. Mikey's been saying for a while now that he's going to die young. It used to be, "Oh, I'm not gonna make it to 30." He's 36 now; so much for that plan. I can't really imagine spending my life with anyone else!

2017

A year ago, Mikey had just started his new job with Avery Brewing Co. It took him awhile to adjust to the different environment and new set of responsibilities; he wasn't sure he'd made the right decision. Since then, he's gotten more comfortable and learned a lot, which makes him feel like he's doing a better job ... which gives him more confidence ... which has in turn helped him and I to get along better at home. He's happier these days, and that helps our relationship in general.

I've found that if one person is experiencing personal (inner) turmoil, no matter how supportive the other partner is and/or how stable the relationship seems to be, that stress is inevitably going to echo into the relationship. If you don't have confidence in yourself at work (or in any other arena), you bring that low self-esteem home with you as well. You might

Jade & Mikey

start to question things you previously felt confident in—like the role you play in your relationship, for example. Unhappiness requires a lot of "emotional tending." It takes so much of your energy that you often don't have any left over for your partner.

What happens is that you start asking more of your partner—and then it becomes draining for both halves of a couple. The partner who is not in the unhappy state wants to support their partner who's struggling, but is not feeling supported themselves. So it can cause some conflict, I think. Mikey goes back and forth. Like all of us, he has good days and bad days, or good phases and bad phases. Alcohol is a demon he will struggle with all his life. It's the case with anyone who has any sort of addiction issues: it's never going to be solid and stable. It's always going to be a bit of a precarious wave. I've had to come to terms with that in our relationship.

It's hard to empathize sometimes because I don't have an addictive personality, so I don't understand where that impulse comes from. I do make sure to call him on it, rather than ignoring the situation—which is its own delicate dance. I have to navigate when to speak up and how to speak up in a way that doesn't just make him pull further away. Of utmost importance is letting him know that my 'interference' originates in compassion. "All right," I say when I see him starting to slip, "you gotta reel it back in before it gets too bad." And I stand my ground on that, while recognizing that addiction is something he fights against; it's not just something he is doing out of irresponsibility or because he's not considering me. Sometimes he can't control it or doesn't even realize that he's doing it. It's a lot easier to see someone else's patterns of behavior.

That's one of the cornerstones of a solid relationship: supporting each other, but also holding each other accountable verbally and consciously. Mikey calls me out on my unhealthy behavior patterns, too, and he's definitely a lot better at the compassion thing than I am. He's a lot more forgiving, probably because he's had more struggles in his life. I'm a little bit Type-A and I hold myself and other people to very high standards. Mikey doesn't have that same uptightness.

Another challenge we've been dealing with this year is financial instability. Mikey took a big pay-cut with his new job, not least of all because he was entering a new industry (which always means starting at the bottom and working your way up again). He'd been a bartender for 15 years. It was comfortable and attractive because the money was just so good. He doesn't walk out of work every day with hundreds of tip-dollars in his pocket anymore; he makes a monthly salary, paid once/month. This scenario requires budgeting skills he's never had to use before. Learning some financial responsibility has been good for him, but ultimately it's been a hard learning curve. We can't and don't spend as flagrantly as we used to. But Mikey is happier—and you can't put a price on that.

Last time I mentioned that the death of Mikey's mom is really what started his drinking. He never really dealt with her death—but is being forced to now that his dad was just diagnosed with lung cancer. They've never had a close relationship, but the idea that he might lose his only living parent relatively soon is making him yearn for a closure that I'm not sure he's going to get. Mikey needs a lot of support right now, and although it's draining me, I'm trying not to close off to him. That's one of my coping mechanisms that I'm aware of—I shut down whenever I start to feel depleted, like, "Nope, I can't take it anymore." That's not fair to him, either, so we've been discussing how we both can feel mutually supported.

Running is one of my self-care practices. I don't like to run with other people; the trail is my private space and I treat it like a moving meditation—a time to think through stuff and clear my head. I also practice yoga, and make sure that I'm eating well and drinking enough water. These simple things, observed on a daily basis, keep me feeling strong and capable.

We've also had plenty of cause to celebrate in 2017. We had cameo roles in a documentary that came out this year about the drinking sport Gelande Quaffing. Mikey was the captain and I was the coach and our team won the 2015 Gelande Quaffing World Championship (held every year in Jackson Hole, WY) . All that year a camera crew followed us around, and in September it's debuting at the Crested Butte film festival. That's pretty exciting because it's something that we've put two years of our lives into with our friends. It cost a lot of money and a lot of physical and emotional stress for both of us, but now it feels like this kind of collective goal that we accomplished—and there's artistic proof! For people who know nothing about the sport, it's a chance for us to gauge the public reaction.

It's been a busy year for me. I tend to take on several projects at once, like teaching and running a non-profit writing collective in addition to my full-time job. I think it's going pretty well, but it's admittedly a lot. One thing I can say for Mikey is that he will never tell me, "You shouldn't take on more, you're doing too much," even though it can be a burden on him. I have all kinds of commitments and not as much free time and I'm always a little stressed out, so he does have to shoulder that. But he's always very supportive, so I appreciate that about him.

In 2018, we hope to travel together more. This January, we're headed to Hawaii. We want to be better about actually taking vacation time and having adventures together. Usually our travels center around weddings or family obligations, so I'm looking forward to doing some more fun stuff with just us!

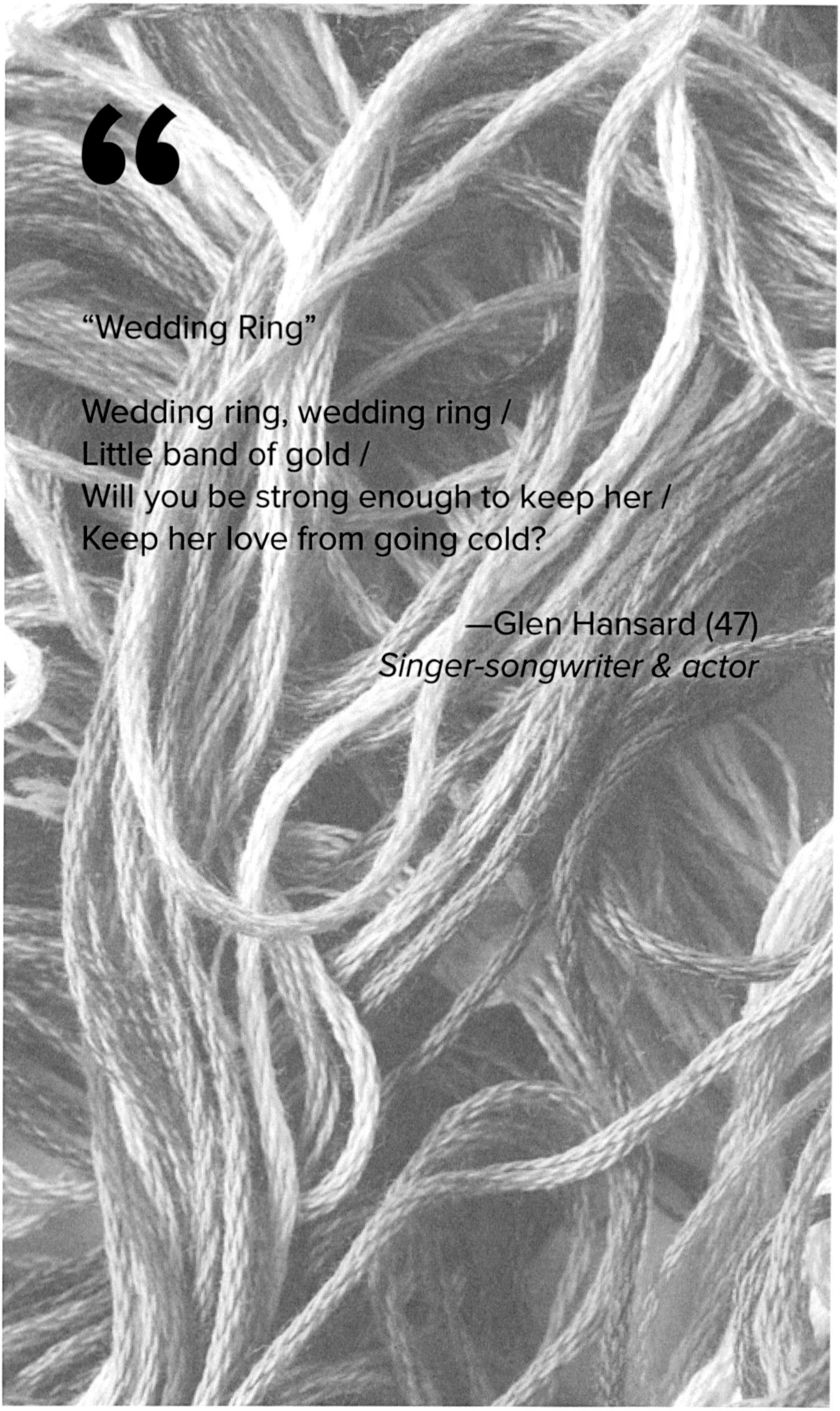

“Wedding Ring”

Wedding ring, wedding ring /
Little band of gold /
Will you be strong enough to keep her /
Keep her love from going cold?

—Glen Hansard (47)
Singer-songwriter & actor

MORGANA & DEVIN

[Morgana (50) is a #1 international bestselling author and the president of Charmed Life Coaching, Inc. A self-described "Money Goddess," she helps entrepreneurs, artists, healers, and humanitarians thrive in their purpose, attract more than they chase, and make things happen with ease, flow, and synchronicity. Her husband Devin (51) is a travel writer and Editor-in-Chief for In the Know Traveler. *Morgana and Devin, who live in California, made a vow to marry 100 times in 100 countries. At time of writing, they've said "I do" 20 times.]*

2016

Devin and I met online, but we lived a few blocks away from each other for 15 years. We went to the same gym, the same market, the same events—and never met. I tease him about why he never hit on me in all that time. He says we never saw each other, which is probably true: I would have remembered a cute face like that.

He messaged me first on OKCupid. I didn't write back immediately because I was dating Kevin the too-young-for-me puppeteer for about two weeks. (Who could have predicted the end of *that* relationship, right? LOL.) Devin almost gave up waiting for me to respond, but eventually I did and we went on our first date. I remember that day I was about six cities away shooting a video for a friend's project, and I got stuck in traffic coming back. I didn't have a chance to go home before meeting him, and tired, I wasn't even feeling the date by then.

Luckily, Devin was a lot cuter in person than in his profile photos, which were all really awful except for this one photo where he's playing guitar in a red plaid shirt and looking off into the distance. I felt really comfortable with him immediately. That first date lasted six hours, we just had so much to talk about. He was interesting and I could be myself with him, which is a big indicator for me. If I am chatty and nervous and trying to impress someone, that's a clue that he's not my guy. When I realized I wasn't putting on a 'show' for Devin, and that I felt safe with him, I decided to go out with him again.

I didn't like him enough by the end of the first date to be having relationship fantasies, and he tells me he felt the same. But he liked that I was a brunette, "smart, funny, and attractive" (his words), and that I was a cheap date. Although we met at an Irish bar near my house, neither of us really drink, so we drank a lot of water and ate pistachio nuts. For six hours.

On our second date, he took me to Griffith Observatory, which is featured in the movie *Rebel without a Cause*. We were up there looking at the stars and I noticed that some stars are kind of white and some stars are kind of yellow. I pointed that out to Devin and he came up with a really bad, outrageous lie to explain it. It was so absurd, but he said it with such conviction that I was totally charmed. That was the moment I started liking him. I fell in love with his ability to lie.

He told me later that he thought he was going to get lucky that night. He didn't.

I was 45 at the time and looking for a serious

relationship. I asked him his views on marriage on our second or third date. He told me he didn't believe in marriage, which is pretty funny for a guy who's getting married 100 times in 100 countries. (That scheme was 100% his idea, by the way. More on that in a second.) Devin had been married before and it hadn't worked out, so he was feeling pretty burned on the idea, but when he found out how important it was to me, he said he could see himself getting married again. He says now that he was totally lying (still hoping to get lucky!) but it was enough for me to keep dating him.[1]

Some little girls come out of the womb dreaming of fairytales and romance, and I was one of them. I chased true love my whole life (starting with chasing Brian Patterson under the piano on his 5th birthday; and Brian was the older man!), yet I'd intentionally never gotten married—because I never wanted to get divorced. I wasn't willing to pretend that a relationship was right when it wasn't. For decades longer than most women my age, I held out for a life partner whom I could love and respect, who would make me laugh, and with whom I could travel the world. I believe life is better in partnership—that when you're with the right person, life is richer. You know, life is rough, but the benefit of being in this bag of skin is that human beings have the capacity to love.

Marriage is so much better than I expected because I didn't know what it would be like. I thought that being married would be the same as being boyfriend-girlfriend. Devin asked me to marry him just 18 months after we met, and while I knew he was The

---

1 I should mention here that even though I talk about Devin lying a lot, he's the most honest person I've met. When he lies it's always a joke, and he's always been trustworthy, which is a big reason I'm with him.

One, he caught me off-guard. I thought we'd date for 4 or 5 years. We both travel a lot for work, and in fact he was in South Africa on a photography assignment and I was leading my goddess retreat in Bali when he proposed to me over Skype.

The story is really Devin's to tell, but basically he was on safari just a few miles from the Botswanan border, literally in the middle of the bush. There were lions and hyenas and packs of wild dogs and every morning at 4:00 a.m. he had to be escorted to the tent where the only computer was so that he and I could Skype. One morning the guard was walking him to the tent and a lion roared—not a mile away, but right there in the dark. As Devin says, "Hearing a lion in the wild is very different from hearing one in a zoo or in a movie." His first reaction was to bolt, but the guard grabbed him and said, "You're food and you have to stay here and not be food."

They made it to the tent, and the guard went to "check out" the lion situation. Devin thought he was nuts, but then he reconsidered his own situation. There he was, waking up before the sun every morning for three minutes of spotty conversation with me halfway around the world. *Why would I be doing this unless I really loved her?* he asked himself. All that week, we'd been arguing. Every conversation started with "I don't think you're the right woman for me," and ended with "But I really want this to work," and meanwhile I was dying inside. On the morning of the lion, he said, "Life doesn't give you a guidebook, and advice from your friends and parents is awful. I don't know what the right thing to do is, but I know that I love you. Will you marry me?"

"What?" I said, sure I'd misunderstood him over the staticky connection. It seemed like such a quick switch. When he repeated himself, I said, "Yes," but inside I was thinking, *Oh shit, this is going to ruin everything.* I didn't think we were ready. We still had a lot to work on as individuals and partners in relationship.

He had another week in Africa and I was busy in Bali, but I found some quiet moments there to reflect on what I really wanted. I ran through my fantasy for the millionth time: the big princess dress; the church; the guest list—and I had this moment of clarity. That's all great when you have parents doing the work and footing the bill, but at 47 it was just me. I thought about how much I hate doing anything like booking hotel rooms or catering (I don't even like doing that for my own events), and I realized that our relationship was the prize. I didn't want or need to drop $70,000 on a bad party when we could put it toward a house instead. All that pomp and circumstance seemed like too much pressure to put on an infant marriage.

So I got home on a Thursday, picked him up on Friday, and we eloped that night. In the same courtroom as Brad and Angelina, if you can believe it. The next day we went shopping for rings. I didn't find one I liked because they were all alike: gold and round and boring. Devin bought his from a jug for $9. It's silver and round and boring. I told him, "It has to be a plain gold band, because that's Jewish." He rightly countered: "But you had porkchops for lunch." I couldn't argue against that, so he bought the ring, and that night I Googled "Claddagh Rings." I remembered a trip I'd taken to Ireland and I thought I would get a Claddagh ring, with the little hands, heart, and crown. The Google search brought up a Celtic cross-inspired ring produced by only one company in Los Angeles. I knew that was my ring.

We drove into downtown Los Angeles and discovered that my ringmaker didn't actually have a storefront. They had a cage with a camera and a shady-looking man at the window. I told him what I wanted. "Give me $200 cash and come back in an hour," he said. They made my ring, and that's what I wear today. Then we had chili dogs for our wedding feast.

Before we posted on Facebook, we called our parents. My father was ecstatic. He'd given up on his "spinster" of a daughter.

Our second wedding happened two weeks after our first wedding. Devin was on assignment in Mexico, and they graciously allowed him to bring his new wife along. We called it our "honeymoon." Or I did. Then we had some downtime and we were walking through Puerto Vallarta with another journalist who has like a million Twitter followers, and we passed by Our Lady of Guadalupe, this super old and beautiful cathedral, and Devin asked, "Why don't we get married again?" I said, "Yeah, let's do it," and the journalist said, "I can preside; I'm ordained." (... In the United States, not in Mexico.)

We marched up to the front of the church. There were some people in the front praying, but no service going on, so Devin and I took off our rings and the journalist started speaking about love. Devin realized there were some things he'd forgotten to mention in our first round of vows; he talked about wanting to give me peace and comfort, and how he hoped to always be a "soft landing" for me. It all felt deeper than our original wedding. And then I was crying and the people in the pews were applauding.

Later, Devin told me: "A wedding day is fantastic

and monumental, but a single moment may or may not continue to carry you through the ages. I think if you continue to make a particular moment special by saying (again and again) how you feel, what you want from the other person, and what you're going to bring to the relationship, then when you leave the front door, you know who's on your team. You know who's going to show up when there's illness or problems with friends or family." We started this ritual where we say, "I love you. This is why: ... and here's what I'm going to do to give you happiness and peace." It renews our sense of security in the relationship, and lets us live our own lives while honoring the love that we have for each other.

Since then, we've married each other 18 times. Once in Bali. Once in Canada. Once in Austin, Texas. Slovenia was probably our most official ceremony. The mayor officiated in his Grand Poobah outfit. He wore a tall hat and robes with a black fur collar that he claimed was cat fur just to horrify me, and he cracked bawdy jokes about first-night privileges. Our whole conversation was mediated by an interpreter. We married in a thousand-year-old Slovenian castle that overlooked a lake and an island. Slovenian tradition dictated that Devin carry me up the 99 Steps of Despair to ensure a long and happy marriage. It was an ordeal. Once at the top, we rang the Bell of Wishes.

Slovenia has been my favorite wedding to date. Devin's was San Marino. He reached out to one of his connections in the publishing world and said, "Hey, Morgana and I are looking to get married in Italy. Can you recommend a shady glen somewhere?" They responded and said, "If you come on this particular day, we will give you an Italian Bvlgari wedding from the

Middle Ages." With costumes. And a castle.

The costumes sold me. My grandmother started a Renaissance fair (which is why I have such a silly name). We had to do it. So we went to San Marino and there were 50 costumed actors, singing and dancing, plus a period recreation of the ceremony. I sat in a tower all day in my medieval underwear, waiting for Devin to send out my shoes and my dress and my jewelry. I had four ladies-in-waiting to dress me and two knights outside the door guarding my purity. The actor who played my father was (in real life) French foreign legion and used to be a bodyguard to the pope. A total badass, he really played it up with the sword.

They're our San Marino family now. We're friends on Facebook, and my "dad" is always posting photos with guns and weapons and I'm a tree-hugging peacenik. It was the most wonderful, generous, crazy experience. Devin looked so handsome in his prince costume. At the end, they knighted Devin, so technically he's a "cavalier de San Marino."

We had a spectacular wedding in Turkey, where I literally rode down the aisle, garbed in traditional Turkish wedding attire, on a horse. That horse had its own horse, so wherever one animal went, the other followed. The Minister of Culture married us in a museum, then the governor invited us to dinner in an 800-year-old mansion. After a dinner of goulash, we holed up in an amazingly romantic cave-like hotel where St. Stephen used to live. It's over 2,000 years old—one of the most romantic hotels on earth! It's located in Goreme, in Cappadocia. You should go.

Not every wedding has been that over-the-top. To most of my weddings, I wore a cute white lace dress that I got at Ross for $20. Our Italian host in

Rome overheard some Italian women saying how much they loved the dress; it was "so much better" than the gaudy satin dresses with the puffy sleeves. There have been times I forgot to pack shoes and I got married in flip flops with bug bites on my legs. Or I lost my brush and had to comb my hair last-minute with the wedding veil. It's not about the glamour. It's about the relationship. It also helps knowing you have 100 chances to get it right. The dress doesn't matter. No one cares if we mess up our vows. We never write them down because they're fresh and new and we know each other better every time.

One of Devin's childhood friends in Serbia asked to have a double wedding with us. I thought, *I have 100; sure, I can share one!* It was a really bad wedding, a mess from the get-go. We lost our ATM cards and were late getting to the venue, so then we had a too-short window for the ceremony. Some day-drinking had been happening, and a few of the guests booed when Devin said his vows. His words were such poetry, I was like, *Are you kidding me?!* Tensions escalated. Then when I threw my bouquet it just landed, thump, three bounces. No one cared. At the end of the evening, Devin told me, "I'm going to get into a fight unless we leave now," so we made a hasty exit.

Ironically, Devin had had an inkling that such tomfoolery might go down before we ever left the hotel, and he'd asked the receptionist while I was getting my hair done if, worst case scenario, someone on staff could marry us later on. She had said, "Absolutely!" and so we took the bus back from Belgrade in the rain, showed up sopping wet in our wedding clothes, and married for the second time that day. We call it Wedding 7A and 7B. (Belgrade, by the way, its citizens notwithstanding, is a great city. We met a very nice woman there named Snow White!)

Why I believe that no one can ruin your wedding is because when it's all said and done, I'm going home with the one person I adore and nobody else. The marriage is the prize, not the party. At our wedding in Laredo, Mexico last year, one of the guests was having a really hard time emotionally. She apologized and said, "Oh, I don't want to ruin your wedding." I had to laugh and tell her about Serbia, and remind us both that the wedding isn't about the day, it's about the relationship. She felt better then and ended up catching the bouquet!

There's no master list for when and where we plan to get married. If we take a trip together or happen to both be visiting the same country on business, you can bet a wedding will take place at some point. We've also had to relax the unwritten 'rules' a bit, like when we got married in Texas even though we'd already married in California. Austin had this really great chapel and several of our friends were there—what are you going to do? I'd never been married in front of so many people I knew.

Another time I was preparing to lead a second retreat in Bali and I just wasn't getting excited. I had all these amazing women signed up; why couldn't I feel enthusiastic? Then it occurred to me: I didn't want to leave my husband. So we bought tickets for him to come with me. We had a wedding there. All the women from the retreat came, which set a certain precedent, because the next time I spoke in Canada they threw a wedding for us in Toronto. That's how the woman asking me to come speak got me to agree. It was super sweet.

The one I'm most excited for in the future is South Africa. I've always wanted to go there, and of course it holds a special place in my heart since that's where Devin proposed. His colleagues there have offered to marry us in a traditional Zulu ceremony. That will be the cherry on top!

It's really beautiful to experience love and love-traditions in other countries. Everywhere we go, people are so warm. Everybody loves love. They're so welcoming and generous; it's like picking up a new family in every country. Especially with the ways things are going politically right now, I've appreciated getting married in three Muslim countries. They're just like us. There's something so healing about getting to experience the humanity of people we're always hearing bad stuff about.

One of Devin's friends always says, "Love is an action and action is service." I think the idea is that to love someone is to want what they want, even when it doesn't serve you. We have to root for each other. Devin is going to make a lot of decisions. Some will be brilliant, some won't be. Same with me—same with all the people we love. My job is to be a support when he doesn't get it right, or it's hard, or it's not convenient. It's easy to be in love when it's convenient. When it's messy and inconvenient—that's when you have to choose to show up anyway, and be a reliable, consistent partner.

Devin and I have a great relationship. We don't fight very often. We try to be nice to each other even when we want to kill each other. Every time we say "I do," we are reminded of what it means to be married: to choose each other over and over again. I think we will reach 100 weddings. It will take a bit of time, but

Morgana & Devin

the countries aren't going anywhere. And then we'll probably start over. Because it's not about the number ... it's about the lifestyle.

2017

How do I feel about Devin today? Oh, I adore him. I'm like super, sickly happy. I love him more as time goes on. It's surprising. After a 45-year track record of perfect failure, I am finally really happy. I'm with someone who is just warm and fun and kind and a really good relationship partner, and who amazingly enough loves me. I'm still a gooey newlywed. What can I say?

2017 has been a challenging year, for several reasons. My grandmother died and my father moved across the country for Alzheimer's care, so it's been a transitional year for me. I'm grateful not to be going through it alone. Not only do I have an incredible partner, but it's lucky that I get along with Devin's mom famously. She owns multiple rental properties and is going to help me fix up Dad's old house so we can either rent it or put it on the market. It's an amazing house, but it's falling apart and needs to be cleaned up. She knows what needs to be done, how much things cost, and who's good. Doing this all by myself, without my love-team, would be kind of terrifying.

Devin's been grappling with transition as well: his daughter left for college this fall, which was especially heartbreaking since they hadn't really spoken for a year leading up to her leaving. It had little to do with him and more to do with her mom, but luckily things are better now. I was struggling, living with a man I love who couldn't always be emotionally present. When she left it was like things 'lightened up,' and it seems their relationship is back on track now.

Some truly amazing things also happened this year. Devin spent many years writing a memoir, and for the longest time nothing was clicking. He couldn't find an interested agent or publishing house—until the month his daughter moved to Michigan. Then he got a book deal! It's called *10,000 Miles with my Dead Father's Ashes*. Imagine a road-trip buddy-movie with your dead dad. It's crazy dark and entertaining and funny and weird. These huge, mega-successful writers are going crazy over it, praising his book and recommending it. I'm so excited for him. I can't wait to help him launch it and market it—anything I can do to contribute!

I've also watched things fall into place for many of my clients this year. We're talking seven and eight figures—millions and tens of millions of dollars, as they wake up to and work through their money blocks. I can't help but believe that the happier and more supported I feel in my own love life, the more that mojo is multiplied to benefit my clients. The arc of client success stories grows bigger and more dramatic with every wedding. Which is not to say that people who don't want to be married and/or who just want to go it alone can't find that same success ... of course they can! I just know I'm a very relationship-oriented person, and kind of an extreme one at that. I was looking for my soulmate when I was four-and-a-half years old. Now here I am, madly in love with my husband and my life.

Inspired by Devin, I wrote my own book proposal in June. It's for a book called *Money Goddess*, which would delve into seven goddess archetypes for feminine, economic, and personal empowerment. I have an agent who's shopping it around right now. Here's to hoping that I'll spend 2018 immersed in the world of writing. There's also an eighth Bali retreat coming up, and of course we want to keep traveling together and get married a few more times—all in between cleaning up and selling Dad's house. So we'll be busy ... but there's no one else I'd rather get lost in those projects with than the man who helps make them possible.

Here's the thing. I was looking for my person forever. Long before I met Devin, I started asking all the long-time married couples I know, "What's your secret?" They all gave me exactly the same answer: "I picked the right person." It's not that you won't have disagreements. It's not that you won't have moments where you want to leave. I'm extremely political and very admiring of Hilary Clinton. My husband is not a Trumper, thank gosh, but he's not on the same page as me. And there are times I get so overwhelmed and upset, I want to jump right out of our moving car. You're going to have that. But our commitment (and recommitment) to our love confirms that I picked the right one for me.

One of the hallmarks of the Right Person is that he sticks around, works it out with you, and is good to you. That's a must-have, not a would-be-nice. As a friend of mine so brilliantly put it, "Look for character, not characteristics." If you're dating someone, don't date his potential. Don't fall in love with who he could be, because that's not who you get. All you get is the person he is right now. Are you okay with XYZ being like it is for the next 20 or 40 years? If not, then move on. Anything less is disrespectful to both of you.

I love my husband as he is. I'm not trying to

change him. You can't love somebody and try to change them. That's a contradiction. But we women love 'projects,' don't we? We see the potential in everybody. It's not a bad thing necessarily, but this super obnoxious, offensive, old guy in a Bali cafe once said the wisest thing to me, and I want to share it with you here. "Women marry men hoping they'll change, men marry women hoping they'll never change, and neither one is going to get what they want." The best way to avoid this catch-22? Marry the one you want, now, for who he is today. Marry him 100 times, may it please you. Do it on the beach in Bali, or the courthouse down the street. Just do it with an open mind and a wide open heart.

[Anyone interested in reading more about Morgana and Devin can visit their website www.InTheKnowBride.com. There, the couple update their progress toward the big 1-0-0, and Morgana publishes blog articles on her favorite topic: advice for a loving marriage.]

“

If you want to have multiple partners (i.e., cheat on your spouse), then why are you bringing God into it? Marriage isn't just something to do. Marriage is a sacred promise to God with your partner. I feel that this has been lost on some of society.

I knew that I would marry Chris when I realized that I could be head-over-heels one minute, and want to throw him out of the apartment the next. There were no fireworks and hearts floating above my head when I realized, but a *Dang, so this is it; I'm here, this is the person that I will be with for better AND for worse.*

For us 30-somethings, rom-coms and Disney set us up to perceive that happily ever after is easy and happens in hours. Greatness takes hard work, and so does a great love.

—Herta (35)
Hairstylist

“

When my husband and I got married, we took each other’s names. I changed my middle name to his last name, and he changed his middle name to my last name.

—Virginia (28)
Grantwriter

ELLEN & PETER

[Ellen (28) married her post-college sweetheart in 2014. They struggled to find a healthy sexual intimacy. When Peter began putting his career before their marriage, Ellen sought a 'friend with benefits'—with Peter's permission.]

2016

There was a time when I couldn't understand how a child could be born out of wedlock. I didn't believe you could have sex outside of marriage. Some of that you can blame on my Christian upbringing, but most of it I brought on myself, internalizing Christian doctrine to the point of worshipping purity. I started wearing a purity ring on my left ring finger in high school. It bore the letters TLW, for "True Love Waits." In college I dated one guy for three years, but I was still a virgin when we broke up so I started wearing the ring again. My dad thought it was weird. I thought it was cool; everyone from Miley Cyrus to the Jonas Brothers was doing it.

Then I went to Singapore to teach English abroad, and that's where everything shifted. I met all these beautiful Buddhist people and couldn't accept the idea that they were going to hell just because they didn't follow Jesus Christ. I let the purity thing go at the same time. I was 22, a new college graduate, and hungry to experience the world. During one of my breaks from teaching, I went backpacking with some new friends and got into a little trouble. Lost my v-card. It was a 'rebellious phase,' I guess, but it continued when I came back. I lived with my parents for a miserable few months, then moved in with a friend in Fort Worth while job-hunting.

On New Years Eve 2011, this friend and I went to a house party with a bunch of people who all happened to be Baylor University alums. I was the only non-Bear except for Peter, my now-husband—so we immediately hit it off over this random thing we had in common. Then we learned that we'd both lived abroad, and had experienced being a minority in another country. We talked about racism and cultural appreciation vs. cultural appropriation, and at midnight we kissed. It didn't hurt that Peter is super cute. He had long hair then—longer than mine, which was shoulder-length.

We exchanged numbers, but I wasn't sure if I would see him again. I didn't want to make the first move. He ended up texting me the next day and we set up a date. We went out for tacos, then went back to my place to watch the *Star Wars* Blu-ray Peter had brought with him. I had never seen an entire *Star Wars* movie and that was kind of a deal-breaker for him, like, *I like this girl but she needs to see* Star Wars. He was disappointed that I didn't really care for *A New Hope*, but he must have overlooked it because we started seeing a lot of each other after that. He was in school and I was working part-time, so we were both pretty free. On Valentine's Day (about a month later) we became exclusive. I was actually kind of considering someone else, but it was less serious, so I committed to being with Peter.

From the beginning, we both found it really easy to be ourselves around each other. Neither of us felt any need to be a certain way to impress the other person. We liked each other just the way we were. He had broken up with a girlfriend a few months earlier and he said I was "refreshing" compared to his past experiences. I'm more low-maintenance, more laid-back. He gravitated toward that quality because he hadn't had it in a relationship before.

Five or six months down the road, my ex helped me get a full-time job with the company that he worked for, which meant that he and I started spending a lot of time together again. It brought up all these unresolved feelings. We'd broken up while I was in Singapore because he'd wanted to Skype every day (meanwhile, I had a whole new world to explore), but I'd always assumed we would continue dating when I got back. The more I was around him, the stronger my feelings for him became—stronger even (or so I thought) than the feelings I had for Peter. Peter and I broke up in month six, and stayed broken up for about three weeks until I realized, *Oh, there really was something there. And I miss it.*

It was the strangest breakup ever. Peter was still living with his parents, and we went for a walk in the park by their neighborhood. We sat down on a bench and discussed our feelings. Both of us felt sad, but then we went and snuggled up in his bed and watched *Star Wars* after we broke up. It was like we needed that time to process it. A few weeks later, we grabbed lunch together and that's when I realized I wanted him back. The feelings I'd thought were there with my ex really weren't; I was idealizing the situation. Peter had cut his hair off and he looked amazing. It was hard to be with him but not be *with* him.

The following night I was downtown at a meeting with my boss, discussing a possible promotion, when

Peter called and said he wanted to talk. "Now's not a good time," I started, but Peter cut me off. "No," he said. "If you're not going to meet me, it's just done." So I left the meeting and we met at my house, where we had one of those all-night talks that rekindled everything. That was September. We got engaged a year later, over a steak dinner that a client had gifted us as a tip. (By this point, I was helping Peter run his software startup.)

Wedding planning in the academic sense didn't appeal to either of us. We had every intention of getting married, but when and where and how was fuzzy. Christmas 2013 we were visiting my folks in Houston, and because all the family kept bugging us about setting a date, I said to Peter later that night. "What if we got married on New Years Eve—two years to the day we met?" I meant that New Years Eve ... just six days away.

In Texas you have to get your marriage license at least 72 hours in advance, so we rushed back home to apply. Everything was closed, of course, for the holidays. We finally got our wedding scheduled with a justice of the peace, who married us on New Years Eve 2013. It was a complete comedy of errors. My family (including my sister) came, his parents (who live in Forth Worth) came, and my cousin was in town, which was nice—but then we forgot the marriage license. My family had to go back to the house and find it, and I was afraid we were going to miss our appointment.

I wore a champagne-colored Betsey Johnson dress that I'd bought at Macy's. It was solid, with a sheer layer of sequins that made it a really great New Years party dress. I happened to have a haircut scheduled for that day, so my hairdresser styled my hair. Peter's best friend took photos. We all went out for dinner afterward. Our parents got us a room downtown, and Peter and I and his best friend and my sister rang 2014 in on Houston Street, people-watching and doing whatever we wanted.

The plan was to have another, more official party with friends, but that never happened. Three years later, we still haven't taken a honeymoon trip.

Peter and I picked out our own handmade rings on Etsy. His is, unsurprisingly, a tribute to *Star Wars*. It gives me instant credibility with any guy he meets, because they're always like, "Wow, you've got a cool wife." I like that we sat down and looked through the rings together. There was no pretense of 'He needs to know what I like.' We've just never played those games, and have always been upfront and honest.

My parents really like Peter. At first they didn't like that he isn't religious, but I think they've accepted him. A year ago, my mom asked, "What happens when you two have kids?" We try to stay away from politics, preferring to agree to disagree. My parents seem a little more relaxed now that their kids are out of the house, and as an adult myself now, I see more 'human' in them than I ever have before. Anyway, Peter and I aren't having kids anytime soon. His software startup bloomed into a full-scale tech company that consumes most of our time these days. We want business to really be booming before introducing kids into the mix.

We're not just husband and wife, we're also business partners; and that adds a whole other layer to the relationship. I was doing media research for major networks when I took over Peter's social media accounts. When I hit the glass ceiling at my job, I quit and went to work full-time for his company. (Coincidentally or not, that's when the business really took off.) Today I do all of our marketing. It's a real family affair.

Where Peter and I struggle to be as egalitarian is in the home. Sometimes I regret that Peter never lived with a partner before me. His mom did just about everything for him, and he wasn't required to take responsibility for himself around the house. I have ended up taking on a more traditional role—cooking, cleaning, paying the bills—in addition to working full-time, which is something I specifically did not want. I saw what that kind of life did to my mother. When we were young she stayed home with us, but later on she got a full-time job and could barely keep up with the laundry. Meanwhile, my dad's only house 'chore' was to mow the lawn. It's a traditional set-up that many will recognize, and that some of us will spend our lives fighting against.

Our first year of marriage felt like one more year of dating, except that now we had a certificate that said otherwise. Year two, things got a little crazy. I was listening to Peter's best friend Jack (ironically, also one of our employees) talk about his sex life with his ex-girlfriend. They'd regularly invited a third party into their bedroom. Jack's stories seemed so exotic (not to mention, erotic). As he talked, I began to envision myself as the third party. For days afterward, I had a lot of questions and a lot of thoughts. One night I mentioned it in passing to Peter. To my surprise, he seemed into it. Not into having a threesome, exactly—but he said he "wouldn't mind" if *I* experimented ... outside of our marriage with someone he trusted, like Jack.

Early on in our relationship, I'd had some health issues that prevented us from being intimate. Explicitly, I had chronic bacterial vaginosis. It was so uncomfortable that we couldn't have sex for months while it cleared up. Almost as soon as I healed, he started drinking alcohol to the point of impotence. Meaning sex wasn't an original part of the Ellen-Peter equation. And we haven't really figured out how to incorporate it since. We have, unconsciously or otherwise, substituted an emotional and an intellectual connection for a physical one, which is only 'enough' for people who are entirely asexual. Which neither of us are.

So, even without my having to ask, Peter graciously gave me his 'blessing' on three conditions. I could hook up with his friend-slash-employee who used to have threesomes, but not with anyone else; he didn't want to know when we were doing it; and he had permission to have a one-night stand (with protection). Those were the only 'rules' so long as he (Peter) always took precedence over this guy (Jack). It was pretty understanding and selfless on my husband's part, and pretty dang thrilling for me. I loved—I love—Peter to pieces. Jack was only ever supposed to be a fun distraction between the sheets.

Anymore, I'm not sure I believe that women at least can separate sex from intimacy. You probably know where this story is going. Yeah. I caught all the feels. Having never been in a situation like that before—or even *imagined* being in a semi-open marriage—I made the mistake of opening my heart and my legs. What started as 'just sex' led to movie nights and cuddle parties and the occasional slip of an "I love you" once Peter started working 80 or 90 hours a week, leaving me lonely and alone. Don't get me wrong. I'm not blaming him. In fact, I admire how passionate he is about his work. But it did take him away from me, and well ... Jack was there.

The night I realized that things had gone too far was the night that Jack ended it. This was just a couple months ago. It was ugly. He said something that hurt my feelings, then I said something that hurt his feelings, prompting him to say, "We're done." My reaction was as emotionally violent as if we had been a couple and were now breaking up. Looking back, I think part of the hurt stemmed from shame at having offended him so deeply, but it's difficult to parse out because he'd been a friend for so long. I've known Jack almost as long as I've known Peter. We're not romantically compatible, only sexually, which should logically rule out my having any feelings. But that's not how feelings work, now is it?

I honored my end of the deal and never saw anyone other than Jack. There were a couple times (that I knew about anyway) that Jack hooked up with other people. It made me irrationally jealous, and there was no one with whom I could work through those feelings. Obviously I couldn't talk to Peter about it, and I wasn't sure who I could trust to keep our secret outside the three of us. How do you just casually mention, 'Yes, I'm married, and I'm also in a relationship?' My best friend is very much like, "You are married 'til death do you part." She wouldn't understand what 'hurt feelings' had to do with anything. Plus, I was always scared that someone else would find out and it would reflect badly on the business. Our reputation is everything we have in Fort Worth.

In many ways, my affair (I hate calling it that; it's not really an affair, but something else that society isn't cool with) was a Band-aid for our marriage. It smoothed over and made a non-issue of the one thing that wasn't in our marriage: sex. But it also stopped us from growing as a couple, because we no longer had to address our problems. The emotional support that I would otherwise have sought from my husband, I could now get from Jack. Especially when the problem I needed support for was Peter. My husband worked so late so routinely ... and buried himself in a bottle every other waking moment ... it's not like I had to 'hide' Jack from him. Peter took care of that by conveniently ignoring the truth. I see now how unfair that was to Peter. Before Jack became my lover, he'd been one of Peter's best friends. By confiding in Jack about Peter, I put him in a position where he had to take sides.

For the entirety of our marriage, Peter has 'managed' his alcoholism by keeping it a secret from everyone who matters. Clients. His family. Some friends. I guess we both have really big secrets. Importantly, we've tried not to let either of our vices impact our commitment to each other. True to his word, Peter has never asked about my relationship with Jack, and I don't judge him when I find half-empty liquor bottles stashed around the house. Dissolving our marriage has not, to this point, been an option. It's hard to remotely consider, given the business we own together and the lives we've built together. Only once did I present Peter with an ultimatum, after he wrecked my car driving drunk in the neighborhood, but it was an empty threat. "I'm not going to sit here and watch you destroy yourself," I said, ever so righteously. But of course I did. And I do. Because I love him.

Do I think marriage is, unequivocally, forever? No. Divorce is often ugly and always unfortunate, but it's the only solution in the case of violence or abuse, whether directed at yourself or your partner. If Peter doesn't get his stuff together and stop drinking, that's where we're headed. It's not something I want, but something I'd see as a necessity. In fact, I think my dad was divorced before he met my mom and never told us. My sister found a marriage license on Ancestry.com and he avoided her questions. All three of his brothers are divorced and my mom's parents are divorced. My parents have a good relationship. They're cute. Dad says Mom is the love of his life. There's some tension sometimes, like when my mom doesn't agree with my dad but won't say anything because he's in charge. I'm pretty sure they'll make it. They've been together 33 years.

It's hard to imagine the next five or 10 years, let alone 33. Our business has doubled each of the last two years. Who knows what it will look like a decade from now? Hopefully it's very successful and our quality of life reflects that. One of my goals is to start a foundation, and use the services we already provide to more directly answer some of the world's problems and positively impact people's lives. Lately I've been feeling more like I don't want kids, which could itself be grounds for divorce—though Peter hasn't given me any indication that he's ever thought of leaving me.

I guess I find it kind of crazy that we sign up for one person to be our everything. It's a totally unfair expectation. Which is why, if Peter wanted to have a similar extramarital relationship with someone, I would accept it. He actually made out with a woman at a SXSW party two years ago and I never would have found out except that he invited her to our business's grand opening party. He failed to tell her that he was married before kissing her, which I chided him for, because she had a right to know and people aren't always cool. Apparently he invited her to the party to introduce her to our friend, but then I found out about them and had to fake my composure (I wasn't 'jealous,' exactly, I just wish he'd told me beforehand) the rest of the time, which wasn't awesome. I don't think he's done anything with anyone else, but I suppose I might not know.

Despite the rollercoaster, at this moment I can honestly say that I'm happy. Peter's drinking has been a little better lately. He's been getting help—taking supplements that curb his cravings and occasionally dropping in on AA. The sting of seeing Jack at work every day is fading. I was depressed when we first ended things—especially since Jack went and found a girlfriend right away. Peter could tell I was hurting and forbade me from seeing Jack after that. "I don't want to see you go through that again," he said. But then just yesterday, actually, he lifted the 'ban.' He seems to think our marriage is better when I'm getting what I need. So it will be difficult to navigate. Should I start seeing Jack again? Will he even have me? I don't know. Being with Jack allowed me to experience something that I'm not able to get in my marriage as often as I'd like. And in a relatively tame way, too. I wasn't sleeping with strangers. I wasn't being unsafe. Yet, my closest bosom buddy was a man who's not my husband.

Before Peter lifted the ban, I was doing some research into which dating sites/apps are the most discreet. I've never used one, but I was thinking about dating a girl—just because I never have, and I'd like to try it. I told Peter that and he said he wants some more time to wrap his head around it. Which is fine. Having one ‘friend’ at a time to deal with is simpler ... even though it’s still very complicated!

2017

So, let’s catch you up. Peter and I are still married. Jack *did* take me back, and I *did* continue seeing him—no girls, or anyone else—for most of the past year. We were on-again, off-again depending on what other commitments took priority in any given month. For example, he traveled out of the country for all of August; I stayed busy at work and didn’t even miss him. But I sure was happy when he came back. At first.

Then Jack told me that he’d accepted a new job, and would be moving across town to better serve his new employer. I’d had such easy access to him when he worked in our office and lived so close. That’s probably been the biggest adjustment for me—having to schedule time and make a conscious effort to see him. We’ve only hung out maybe three times since he moved. Peter is still working really late a lot, and I miss Jack’s built-in companionship. There might be three or four hours most days between the time that I get home and Peter gets home, and then he usually goes straight to bed. I’m lonely. It’s making me depressed. I need to be better about asking girlfriends to hang out; honestly, I should be out networking, but I haven’t been in the mood.

It’s probably for the best. Things changed with Jack this year. The way he started treating me (less like a bosom buddy, more like a booty call) caused me to re-examine what I believed to be my ‘love’ for him. He was happy to be a warm body, but if I needed anything more from him—any kind of emotional support—it felt like he played along for what it could get him: namely, sex. Like his actions were calculated, performed 'in exchange for,' while always putting himself first. I still consider him a friend. I still like him. I'm just more aware of our relationship as it is, compared to what I thought it was.

Plus, there's Peter to think about. He's once again decided that he's uncomfortable with our 'arrangement.' The last time I saw Jack, he came over to the house on a Saturday that Peter was working. When Peter came home, he asked what I'd done that day.

"Slept, mostly," I said. "Oh, and Jack came over."

Peter froze. "Just to say hi?" he asked too nonchalantly.

"Not exactly."

I could tell Peter was trying to fight back tears. He wasn't as okay with the whole situation as he'd led both me and himself to believe. He'd also violated our Don't Ask, Don't Tell policy. That wasn't my fault and he knew it, but he didn't know what to do next. After he yelled for me to "Get the fuck away," I went for a walk around the block. When I got back, he was gone. I could see on our office alarm app that he'd gone to work, but he wouldn't answer my calls and texts. Unsure what to do myself, I asked Reddit.

Several months earlier, I'd found the endless rabbit hole that is Reddit by Googling "How to get my cat to stop bullying my other cat." It was while clicking through from one article to another that I found the non-monogamy thread. The "alternative marriage" underground. On the afternoon that Peter disappeared, I added my first post to the thread: "This is what happened ... is there something I can do to fix it?" No one had replied by the time Peter came home. He apologized. Said he'd left because he'd been angry and hadn't wanted to take it out on me. That he's "not okay with everything," the way he'd tried to be. That anymore, he just felt "obligated" to be okay. I deleted my post.

We spent the next day together, reconnecting, even paying a visit to our favorite adult toy store. There we got some CBD lube. (CBD is the other compound in weed that's not psychoactive. You can take CBD and drive; it just helps you relax and aids in pain relief.) Let's just say we found a better appreciation for each other that day.

Peter still drinks, albeit less. For a while he gave up alcohol entirely, but started smoking cigarettes to replace it. He's constantly replacing the vices he's quitting and it doesn't feel like a net gain. Every week is something different. I'm waiting for the week when he says, "I'm not trying to stop anything anymore." At time of writing, his habit is to 1) drink; 2) feel guilty about drinking; 3) go to work to 'make up for' the drinking (productivity-wise); 4) be unproductive/ineffective at work; 5) waste the whole day; 6) not spend any time with me.

He says he "just wants us to have a more stable foundation." But we're forever on the cusp of Almost There and Things Will be Great. Then there's another crisis (like Jack quitting unexpectedly) and we're back to square one, which could very well be the story of our lives as entrepreneurs.

I haven't looked for anyone else to replace my vice. I haven't wanted to look. Jack was so convenient; that I knew him made it that much easier. I hadn't realized at first how subconsciously attracted to him that I am because, like a good wife, I'd blocked off that part of my awareness. Given that I don't know that many people to begin with, I don't have a subconscious longing for anyone else. Peter hasn't seen anyone else that I'm aware of either.

Our goal for now is to focus on each other more. When we actually spend time together, it's really awesome. I still want to make us work. We just bought tickets to Denver for early March. I had credit that was going to expire so we got a really good deal. We're hoping to ski or snowboard. Neither of us has done that before, so we'll learn together. And smoke. It's Colorado, after all.

It feels like we're each doing a little better every day, though it's a lot of work. He's got his issues and I've got mine, but we're trying to figure it out.

“

Emily [my wife] is very self-sufficient. She would rather be alone and happy, than with someone and unhappy. So, I work to bring something positive or meaningful to her life. She does the same for me. We both seek to add something to each other’s lives. We both seek to bring our best selves to the relationship.

—David (43)
Entrepreneur

BRENDAN OWENS

[Brendan Owens, M.A., is a licensed marriage and family therapist at C2 Change in West Austin. He works with couples and families of all stripes who want to improve their relationships. "The number one roadblock to healthy relationships," says Brendan, "is effective communication."]

Couples seek therapy for many different reasons, but almost all of them express a desire for better communication. It has been my experience that 'communication' means different things to different people; allow me to offer a few definitions.

According to the Oxford Dictionary, 'communication' first entails "the imparting or exchanging of information or news." Two people rely on this form of communication when attempting to coordinate their lives in a satisfying and harmonious manner—for example, when deciding what to cook for dinner, or what to watch next on Netflix. When couples need assistance in this area, we practice clear, confident, and non-confrontational self-expression, as well as active listening skills.

More often, however, the request for 'better communication' points to something deeper. The Oxford Dictionary offers this second definition for communication: "a means of connection between people." While this interpretation feels closer to what my clients are looking for, 'connection' can be an equally ambiguous term. How do we feel when we are connected to others? My research and experience indicate that people feel most connected when they feel safe, heard, and understood. 'Understood' is not the same as being in agreement; you and I can disagree and still feel connected so long as we can "exchange information" without fear of judgment. The quickest way to elicit an unkind response is to judge.

That said, 'connection' does not happen automatically. Many couples struggle to connect without the tools to do so. Most of us learn our communication style from our family of origin and we depend on that style as we enter adulthood. Therapists can identify each party's communication style and how it fits with their partner's. It is not only what we say and how we say it—but the story we are telling ourselves as we listen to our partner speak. My job during any therapy session is to create a space for each person to speak, stripping away judgment, assumptions, and mind-reading.

Recently, I was working with a couple having a tough time in their relationship. (Lots of arguing without knowing what the argument was about.) Like many couples, they decided to enter therapy as a last resort. The wife had grown up in an orphanage. While self-reliant and driven as an adult, she was nevertheless primed for her husband to leave her. Every mistake or misstep was "evidence" that he would abandon her. The husband grew up in a home with an emotionally abusive father. He believed that he could "never be good enough," and interpreted his wife's reactions as proof that he wasn't good enough. These two people loved and cared for each other, but could not stop hurting each other by virtue of their communication styles.

Learning to communicate better—in an open,

honest, nonjudgmental fashion—takes time and hard work, and often the assistance of a therapist (which can be expensive). Luckily, C2 Change makes couples and family therapy available to segments of the population who could not otherwise afford it. So, come visit us! Investing in your relationships always pays enormous dividends for you, your partner, and if applicable, your children.

And if you're not in Austin, here are four techniques to try at home to foster better communication.

ONE

Read Gary Chapman's *The Five Love Languages*. It's a good tool to get both couples and families thinking about how they show and feel love. Whether its acts of service, words of affirmation, quality time, physical touch, or giving gifts, understanding the five love languages is an easy way to start the conversation around giving and receiving love.

Once you know what your partner prefers, you can identify stumbling blocks to good communication. For example, if your partner gives and receives love through physical touch, but you realize that you don't like giving hugs, you can begin to find the compromise or middle ground. Don't go against your values, but if you know your partner would appreciate it, you might try simply holding hands more often.

TWO

If physical touch *is* your love language (or at least something you'd be open to experimenting with), try regularly incorporating full chest-to-chest hugs into your routine. I recommend that couples greet each other this way the first time they see each other every day. Hug, then remain hugging until both of you physically 'soften.'

Researchers at UCLA have studied the science behind hugging—specifically how hugging affects the human nervous system. Full chest-to-chest hugs align two individuals' nervous systems and can help bring them closer to balance, especially when one partner is more excited or upset, and the other partner is calmer.

When a five-year-old drops his ice cream cone or scrapes his knee, the best way to soothe him is to give him a hug. You don't need to scold him and remind him that he was warned not to run. Hugging the child lets him know that you see him, hear him, and have empathy for him—and it works the same way with your partner.

Human bodies are wired for physical touch. If your partner is touch-averse, it might indicate a sensory issue, a trauma, or simply point to how she was raised. Hugging was not part of our communication style in my large Irish Catholic family, so I've had to learn it as an adult.

THREE

To diffuse a tense situation, try having both parties sit back-to-back. It's not important that your backs touch, so long as you can't see each other. One person begins by telling their side of the story. Then s/he should ask their partner, "Did I get that story right?" and allow time/space for the other person to speak. Removing visual triggers like body language and the faces we consciously or unconsciously make can make communication less activating and make it easier to hear our partner's words.

FOUR

Finally, practice nonviolent communication: a four-step process otherwise abbreviated NVC. The first step is to observe what you see without using any judgments or mind-reading. Step 2 is to describe the feeling(s) that your observation evokes. Next, voice a need that you have that's not being met because of the situation. Finally, make a reasonable request of your partner. *Note: a request is not a demand; you must be okay with your partner choosing not to abide by your request.

Consider a situation in which a wife works significantly more hours than her husband. He could berate her and make demands, like: "You need to come home right away after work every night." Or, he could try NVC.

Using NVC, the husband observes: "When I come home after work, you're not here." He continues: "It makes me feel sad and lonely." After contemplating his unmet need, he voices: "I have a need for connection and creating a home together. I want to share my time with you." He ends by reasonably proposing: "Could we figure out a couple days/week that you could leave work at a certain time for us to be together?"

Happy communicating!

[from *Frida*]

I don't believe in marriage. No, I really don't. Let me be clear about that. I think at worst it's a hostile political act, a way for small-minded men to keep women in the house and out of the way, wrapped up in the guise of tradition and conservative religious nonsense. At best, it's a happy delusion—these two people who truly love each other and have no idea how truly miserable they're about to make each other. But, but, when two people know that, and they decide with eyes wide open to face each other and get married anyway, then I don't think it's conservative or delusional. I think it's radical and courageous and very romantic.

—adapted for the screen by Clancy Sigal, Diane Lake, Gregory Nava, and Anna Thomas from the book *Frida: A Biography of Frida Kahlo* by Hayden Herrera.

“

For a long and happy marriage, laugh every day with your best friend (which better be your spouse). Humor is the most effective tool for diffusing anger, venting frustration, and graciously admitting screw-ups.

—Dari (63)
CEO

ROBERT & MARLA

[Robert (41) and his wife of seven years, Marla (41), married in the park on a sunshiny, blue-sky day. Everything was going swimmingly until Robert's increasing anxiety triggered Marla's cold indifference. "I don't know how much longer I'll be married," he sighs.]

2016

I was a high school junior the first time I met Marla, but I wouldn't see her again for 15 years. We had one fleeting hi-how-are-ya on a Dallas-Forth Worth-area campus—lasting ten seconds at most—and the next time I saw her, we'd both aged a decade and a half. The second time we 'met,' Marla showed up at the bachelor party for my brother-in-law-to-be (incidentally, one of her good friends), and we reconnected over craft drafts in the beer garden. Was it the beer, or was Marla flirting with me? I didn't think much of it until she sent me a Facebook friend request, sometime after the bachelor party and before my sister's wedding. From her profile, I learned that she was 32 (same as me) and single.

Marla hadn't been invited to the wedding, but on a whim we threw a little after-party (once my sister and her new husband had been seen safely to the airport), and again, Marla spontaneously showed up. Secretly, I'd been hoping she would come. Later I found out she only came because she thought I would be there. We talked some more and although it felt like we were really clicking, I played it slow. My last relationship had been brutal and toxic; I'd asked the woman to marry me out of desperation (I saw the relationship failing and thought it would be a way to save it) and I was in no rush to make the same mistake again. I didn't ask Marla out. I didn't even ask for her number. Used to getting what she wanted, Marla quickly grew impatient. She told a friend, "If he doesn't get my number at the show next week, I'm done."

"The show" was my show—my indie-rock band's set at an east Austin bar. My keyboardist happened to be one of Marla's high school friends, so she let me know she'd be attending. Between setup, playing, and break down, there wasn't a lot of time to chat. I didn't ask her out, but I did send her a Facebook message two days later: "Hey—just wondering if you want to go for a drink sometime?" We agreed to meet at The Highball (a bar attached to a local cinema chain), where we shared a couple beers.

Not a bad start, but then came the holidays. Christmas and New Years with family and friends made it hard to set anything up. Sometime in January 2009, Marla's brother came to Austin for a concert and invited us to go with him. She and I kissed that night. We officially-unofficially started dating. In her words, she wanted to keep things "very informal," which was fine with me since I wasn't ready to jump into anything. But after a couple months, things started to feel more serious and we had a conversation about it. She asked me to come to Florida with her for a week-long continuing education course she had to take, and that's what launched us into exclusivity. It was the first time we had traveled together, and we had so much fun that we decided to plan several more trips after that.

... Which meant meeting Byron, Marla's ten-year-old son from her first (brief) marriage. She had been very careful about keeping us apart at first. Byron is on the autism spectrum, and for that reason and more she wanted to protect him. We actually met accidentally one time, when my brother and I were at the grocery store. I saw Marla and Byron down the next aisle and waved; she became flustered and embarrassed, and I would only formally meet her son about a month later, on a group vacation to California with Marla's sister's family. Then I invited Marla and Byron to New York City for my cousin's wedding, but ten days before we went Marla's sister-in-law died. The whole family flew in and gathered at her brother's place. There's something about tragedy that brings people closer together: I really became part of the family during that surreal week. Marla wasn't sure she felt up to the wedding after that, but her other brother convinced her it would be good for her to go, and we enjoyed ourselves as much as we could in death's shadow.

In October 2010 I got a promotion at work and started saving money toward a ring. We'd been dating less than two years, but things felt pretty permanent despite our best intentions. I remembered that she'd once pointed out a ring she liked in a jewelry store. When I had enough saved up I went and bought it. Then I asked her over to my apartment, told her to close her eyes, got down on one knee, and proposed. Marla was surprised. Like, incredibly surprised. I specifically avoided any type of spectacular gimmicks because I didn't think she'd like that and I'd heard that marriages that start off like that don't last too long, since you're continually having to go above and beyond for the person. There were no fireworks or choreographed dancers. I just told her how I felt.

Marla said yes and seemed super happy. She'd started to think I wasn't interested in marriage. I explained how after my previous relationship, I'd been so insecure in who I was for the longest time that it'd made me unfortunately socially awkward, but adamant about waiting for someone who liked me for me (and who I also liked). I'd done a lot of soul-searching and worked on the parts of myself that I didn't like—including the fact that I suffer from anxiety—until I liked myself. "And that self-actualization process," I said, "brought me you—this beautiful, smart, super rational person; someone aligned with what I want in life, and who has her shit together, too." She embodied care and respect—two of my guiding principles that I borrow from secular humanism (the idea being that you offer your care to people when they need it and want it, but can also step away and respect people when they don't need you to interfere). Marla called the same terms "kindness" and "courtesy." Truly, she was one of the most compassionate, empathetic individuals I'd ever met. Having found her, I was determined to hold on to her 'til death do us part—or for at least as long as she'd have me.

My parents liked Marla from the moment they met her. In fact, they tell me that of all the spouses in the family, they like her the best. She's just very easy-going and unintentionally funny sometimes. The first words she ever said to my parents were "Shut up." They invited us over for dinner, and Marla was so nervous that when my mom opened the door and said, "It's snowing back home," she replied, "Shut up!" They didn't care. They liked her immediately and sometimes I think they like her more than me.

One of my first follow-up questions to Marla after "Will you marry me?" was "When should we tell Byron?" The woman I'd previously been engaged to had also had a kid—a daughter—and I knew that could make things tricky. When I'd first found out Marla had a kid, I'd even wondered *Can I do this again?* Because if it doesn't work out, you're basically breaking up with a whole family. Marla had assuaged those fears early on by saying, "Too many parents put their kids first. At a certain point in your life, you have to put your kid second for a moment so you can develop relationships with other people." It sounds bad, but it's actually not. Your kids aren't your friends; they're your kids. Sometimes you have to focus on your personal life in order to provide your kid a more stable environment. "So," she replied, "I will talk to Byron, but I want to make it clear that he doesn't control my actions and you don't have to get his permission."

There were times after Marla and I got engaged that Byron and I would have an argument and he'd tell his mom, "I don't want you guys to get married." But then, two days later, he'd be like, "I want Robert to go with me to Gattiland (a pizza chain in Round Rock)." One Saturday he didn't tell me he wanted to go to Gattiland, so I settled in to watch a football game and he got so mad he started screaming. We went the next day instead and he loved me again. The photo booth strip still hangs on our fridge. It's hilarious, because in each photo I was like, "Now we're going to be sad. *Snap*. Now we're going to be angry. *Snap*," but people on the spectrum interpret emotion differently, and the faces Byron made look so funny. For sure, Byron's special needs gave me pause whenever I imagined a future with Marla. I wanted to make sure I could handle it, and that he wanted me in his life, too.

If he had concerns, I wanted to address them. We've had our share of challenges, but today I love him like my own son.

He doesn't call me Dad because he has his biological father (who, thankfully, I actually get along with), but he calls me "Pops." This morning I was worried we were going to be late getting to the bus and I said, "Why don't you go ahead and go? I'll get my coffee and catch up."

"No," Byron said. "I don't want to go without my Pops."

So we have these amazing moments, but I'd be lying if I said it's easy being a stepfather.

Marla and I married six months later, in April 2011. She wanted an outdoors wedding, which ruled out May-September in Austin. In April it's just starting to get warm. As it turned out, we picked the perfect day. The skies were overcast when we woke up, but cleared by mid-morning. We exchanged vows in the park, all wildflowers and white-columned buildings. People always say, "My wedding day was the best day of my life; it was magical!" I'm not that type of person, but it was pretty awesome to have everybody we loved there, celebrating our lives for one incredible evening. During one special part of the ceremony, I presented Byron (one of my groomsmen) with an engraved keychain, which really affected people. A friend of my wife's said later, "If I ever have a kid, and something happens to me, and my spouse meets somebody else, I want the ceremony to be like that!" Someone else said it was the best wedding they'd ever been to—which was ironic for me, a guy with anxiety who spends all his time worrying.

We're both atheists, so the ceremony was nonreligious but made possible by family and friends. My brothers served as groomsmen. My sister, who was seven months pregnant at the time, got certified so she could officiate. Marla's brothers played the music. Every niece and nephew except for one nephew who was a baby had a role. There were two ushers, two flower girls. I wore a bespoke suit and she wore a dress that had long been in her family. Her wedding ring matched her engagement ring and her unique sense of style. My ring is from *Lord of the Rings*, dark script and all. She thought I'd like it because I'm such a nerd and I'm so into fantasy literature. I originally saw the rings as an obligatory gesture, more than representing a "sacred bond," but it ended up having more meaning for me than I realized. I didn't expect anything about the day to feel as profound as it did.

Having spent all our money on the wedding, we couldn't afford a honeymoon right away. We went to Oregon in July: flew into Portland, then followed the Hood River to the coast. I wanted to stop in Tillamook because I'd heard of Tillamook cheese, but it was a crap hole. Nothing there. We found one restaurant with a chef from Portland, where we ate lunch. The waiter overheard us talking about the crappy hotels we'd booked, and knowing we were on our honeymoon, said, "Hold on a second. My aunt has an A-frame in Oceanside. She'd be willing to rent it to you for cheap." We woke up the next morning in this giant A-frame with floor-to-ceiling windows overlooking the waves and the rocks and the lighthouses. We drank our weight in craft beer, visited Powell's Books, made some new friends, and I even reconnected with a cousin whom I hadn't seen in years. It wasn't a traditional honeymoon to somewhere tropical, but it was ours.

Sometime after the honeymoon, I started wearing my wedding ring on my right hand. Marla was afraid I would get a bee sting or something and they'd have to saw my finger off, leaving me unable to play guitar. A while later, it migrated from my right ring finger to my right pinky finger. "Why are you wearing your ring on your pinky finger?" she asked once she noticed.

"Because I'm fat. Okay?"

"I didn't say that!" she insisted. "You need to get it resized."

And I do. The ring is too small for my ring finger but too big for my pinky finger, and sometimes it slips off. One time it fell off when I was doing laundry and I couldn't find it. I freaked out because by that point our relationship had become more fraught, and I'd developed this superstition that *As long as I have it on my finger, we'll still be together*. Seeing my finger naked like that was like seeing my relationship fall apart. I found it, later, in the laundry room. It was hiding inside a sock. So I guess you could say my relationship is in a sock at this point.

It's hard to pinpoint the start of our decline. The first year of marriage was really great. We'd bought a condo together just before we tied the knot, so unbeknownst to my Catholic conservative parents, we were already living together and had experienced life under the same roof. I felt like I had realistic expectations going into marriage about what it would be like—which is to say, more or less what things had been like before we got married. But they weren't, due to several uncontrollable and unforeseeable factors. First, my promotion at work (that had paid for Marla's ring) made my life a lot harder. I had a target on my back, which disrupted my sleeping, which started causing health problems and ramping up my anxiety. Weekends became my refuge. At 2:00 on Sunday afternoons I would get sick to my stomach thinking about going back to work the next day. Then I became depressed over (still) not making enough money. Marla wasn't pressuring me, exactly, but I felt this societal pressure bearing down on me all the same: I had a family to provide for now, and even though Marla worked, too, our success rode completely on my shoulders. Or that's how it felt.

Perhaps it's hereditary. For most of his life, my father had extreme anxiety problems, same as me. After he married my mother, he was the only person making money and he was worried that he wouldn't be able to pay for everything. But he didn't tell my mom because 'men' weren't 'supposed' to do that. He would wake up crying in the middle of the night and hide his chest-seizing panic attacks. When Mom finally caught on, she wanted to do everything she could to help him. To share some of the burden so he didn't feel that way. With Marla ... I feel personally blamed for my anxiety. Anxiety is biological. You're born with your brain chemistry. Like any other mental health problem, it's not my fault. What is up to me is how I deal with it.

I have an acknowledged tendency to lash out in anger when I get really frustrated or really stressed. I can pretty quickly get over it—like, in 30 seconds to a minute—because that's how I was raised. In my family, we yelled and screamed for a minute and then we apologized and moved on. Marla grew up differently. She had a manipulative father who "lashed out" in a passive-agressive way, and sometimes I think she expects the same of me. She actually admitted a couple of weeks ago in counseling that her relationship with her father has colored our relationship. My short fuse, combined with my anxiety, created the perfect storm. I relied on poor strategies to "manage" my stress, until finally I had a full-on panic attack. I acted in ways that I'm not very proud of, saying and doing things that made me wonder who I was when I looked in the mirror. Those are the things that pushed me to get help, and to start seeing first a therapist and then an anxiety specialist.

We lived in the condo for two years before moving into a house. Around that time Byron started maturing into a young man, and we experienced all the benefits—and all the teenage angst—that transition brought with it. While I never stopped loving him, there were certainly days I didn't like him, until one day I saw him as a peer. Our interests began aligning. We could hold full-length, adult conversations. He's always been super verbose and smart; suddenly, I found a new appreciation for his crazy imagination and bonkers theories. I realized that my day was bad if I didn't get to talk to him for a little bit, and furthermore, that he could turn a bad day at work into a great evening at home.

I started to think about having another kid. Marla's a great mom. When we talked about it, she said she'd be open to it. But at the time that we decided to try, things were going poorly in our relationship and it never happened. It makes me sad. I've become so accustomed to it that it doesn't make me sad like it used to, but I look back at that time with confusion and frustration.

To me, it feels like Marla's given up on the relationship. She's still 'there,' and says she's rooting for us, but inside it seems that she's thinking, *Too little, too late*. Sometimes she looks back on our marriage and remembers all the good things about it, only to conclude, "I wonder if that's just nostalgia and all that's gone?" She's so busy these days. She only comes to my shows sporadically. We don't even watch TV together anymore. She can't muster enthusiasm for spending 'quality time' together when she feels like it's going to be the same old story. While I'm working on myself every day, our future success rides on whether Marla can forgive me for lashing out like I have. If she can, then we'll carry on. If she can't, we'll probably split up.

My parents are the best example of a successful marriage that I've ever seen. I know a lot of people say that, but having witnessed a ton of relationships, I can say without a doubt they were able to make it work like no one else. They met through their church almost 50 years ago and still feel pretty much the same way about each other as they did on their wedding day. It's evolved, of course, but they still care so much and so deeply. My mom and dad don't have many friends, but my dad always says, "I don't need a lot of friends because your mom is my best friend." I like that my parents have a lot of respect for each other but aren't afraid to show their love through sarcasm, either. It's important to have a sense of humor and be real. In a weird way, when my dad makes fun of my mom, he's really just making her the focus. Marla doesn't appreciate that. She sees sarcasm as criticism—which, again, stems from her relationship with her dad.

When someone asks my dad how long he's been married, he says "84 years. 42 for her, and 42 for me." That lighthearted joking-ness is, to me, the ideal. But I don't think it's achievable in this day and age, because the ways that people meet each other and the ways we view marriage have changed so much. Niklas Luhmann wrote this treatise called *Love as Passion* (1986) in which he lays out how people used to marry for more 'practical' reasons than the lofty ideal of 'love.' Love and respect were fostered over time. [Note: I'm not talking about forced marriages or child brides here. I understand that those were common practices back in the day, and that they still happen outside this country regularly. I'm talking about two people coming together of their own accord and saying "Yes" to a lifelong commitment.] A couple did everything they could then to make it work. There was a much higher threshold for Acceptable Reasons to Break Up, and they were all serious matters, like abuse.

That's not how it works anymore. Now people want a Big Love. They want their One—their soulmate. No one asks, "Does this situation make sense for me?" They jump in headfirst no matter what and worry about the details later. Part of it has to do with Gen X's snowflake sensibilities. We were told that we are special and can do anything, and it's not true. We can do a lot, and perhaps rise above our humble origins, but really we're just self-entitled fools. We want the movie relationship: conflict, resolution, climax, happy ending. Those things were more achievable in the past because people bought into unwritten social contracts about marriage: you get married, so you give up other aspirations or temptations. Now it's about being "happy"—which is all good, except that it makes you stop buying into your marriage. You think, *I don't have to do that if I don't want to; I can do whatever I want.* People are much more willing to give up after a shorter period of time if things aren't going their way. Me included.

We used to talk about the seven-year itch. Today it's the three-year glitch. I don't know how anyone makes marriage work; I find it astounding that my parents have made it 50 years. I realize that if I want my marriage to last, I have two choices: I can adjust my expectations, or I can change myself. Most people don't want to do either. Why adjust your expectations when you can find someone who meets them somewhere else? Why change yourself when you're a snowflake, perfect just as you are? I don't think marriage is dead, but for these reasons I do think it's on life support. It can't be about both happiness and compromise, when one encourages selfishness and the other demands selflessness.

2017

A couple of months ago, Marla got the shock of her life. Her dad died very unexpectedly. Equally unexpected was how much his death affected Marla. They had such a strained relationship that I thought she'd be a little freaked out, but nowhere near an existential crisis—which is what we're dealing with now. It's the loss of potential—the relationship that could have been—that's weighing so heavily on her. For the first few weeks, Byron and I basically had to take care of her, the house, and everything else, because she was incapable of doing anything other than commuting to work and back. The rest of the time she just laid around and cried. I tried to be understanding. I did my best to give her what she needed (namely, those fundamental qualities: care and respect!)—but I struggled with what to say to her and when. If our relationship was already on thin ice, it became precious eggshells overnight.

It's something our couple's therapist probably could have helped us to navigate, if we were still seeing her. But we stopped after Christmas, mainly due to money. I still go to my therapist and she sees one, too. Plus Byron is in therapy, so we just couldn't afford anything else. Even so, one aspect of our marriage has been getting better: we don't argue like we did. That's thanks to a concerted effort on both our parts, and some really helpful strategies to curb my reactivity that I learned in counseling. Part of it though is that I just stopped caring so much about things that really used to bother me. Like sex. We're 41 years old and we haven't had it in two years. Sure, people's sex lives drop off as they age, but even if I was 61 that would still seem like a really, really long time to be abstinent to me. At 41, I should still have an enjoyable sex life with the person I love; but I don't, and it pretty much makes me unhappy every single day.

Still, I decided it doesn't help, when you're trying to fix a problem, to just keep bringing the problem up. Saying, "We gotta work on it, we gotta fix it" just makes it worse. I just let the issues go now, whereas before I would have said, "Hey, I think we need to talk about this because it's upsetting to me." That's no way to resolve the problems, of course, but doing so takes both people, and I can't just keep banging my head against the wall.

I've never seriously thought about cheating. Occasionally I'll muse: *What would it be like if I cheated?* And then I think: *I'm a Boy Scout; I couldn't do it.* I wouldn't even be able to initiate the process. As shy and nervous as I am, entering a relationship of any kind with someone is such a huge deal for me that cheating just wouldn't happen.

Time is almost up for Marla to decide our fate. Byron is now a senior in high school. Assuming he gets accepted to one of the east coast colleges he wants, when he leaves the last tenuous thread holding us together will break. We've done a great job putting him first, and giving him the stable adolescence he deserved. But that responsibility ends on his 18th birthday. I want for this last year of his life with us to be on solid footing; Marla and I shouldn't derail that. Once he's living on campus, however, the chances of our (possible? likely?) divorce impacting him go down and his ability to cope with it goes up.

Byron went to Europe for two months this summer and his absence drove home to me how different things will be when he's gone. In some ways life was easier—one less person's schedule to work around and needs to meet. But I thought it could be a time for Marla and me to reconnect … and instead, it was hard to get her to do anything with me. Then it was my birthday weekend, and usually we all go out to celebrate each other's birthdays, but this year we made it through almost the whole weekend and no one had said anything about my birthday. So late Sunday afternoon, when we were out taking the dog for a walk, I suggested we stop by this Italian gelato place. Byron and Marla didn't want to. "Please?" I begged.

"Okay," they said, "but we're not getting anything."

Of course when we got there, Byron went right up to the counter and ordered, but then they wanted to keep walking instead of sitting down and enjoying, and once again I had to ask, “Can you guys please just come over here?”

They acted really upset with me, but I was the one who was seething under the surface. Back in the car, Byron asked, “Why are you so upset? Why did you get mad that we didn’t want ice cream initially?” I tried really hard not to be that person, who whines and says, “You guys aren’t doing anything for my birthday.” But then Marla jumped on board. “Yeah,” she parroted. “Why are you so upset?”

“I ... just thought that we would do something for my birthday. Normally we go get coffee, or go to see a movie, and do things centered around the birthday person.”

Somehow it got turned around on me. Marla flipped out and started blaming me. “You should have told me,” she insisted. Later, she admitted that she had dropped the ball, but it did little to make me feel better.

It hurt because I’m always trying to do things for my family ... the little things, which can make all the difference. They often go unnoticed, and that’s okay—it’s part of being an adult. But then when I’m accused of not doing much for my family, it makes me feel even more unappreciated. Which is all to say there are still plenty of unresolved issues at this point, and unless something drastic changes, I don’t think we’ll stay together after Byron leaves. I still love my wife. Only, the longer that our non-relationship drags on, the more resentment I feel. It’s inevitable when you’ve put every waking moment into making sure that your faults aren’t the wedge between you, and your spouse knows it, but doesn’t really care.

Another issue affecting our relationship this

year—well, and I wouldn't even say 'issue,' because really it was an accomplishment on my part (one that, again, went unnoticed)—was my fear of flying. I have an extreme fear of flying, and it's always crippled my relationship with Marla, since it makes taking family vacations a whole lot harder. 2017 marked my parents' 50th wedding anniversary, and that's really significant. Important enough for me to want to be there to celebrate it with them. They booked a cruise around the east coast of Canada, leaving from Montreal. I bought a ticket from Austin to Montreal, then immediately scheduled an appointment with a new anxiety specialist to work explicitly on this phobia. We started well in advance—almost 18 months before the trip. He helped me process the trauma that had initially triggered the phobia. (In 2003, I was on a plane to Detroit and we got struck by lightning. The plane was basically flying sideways and I was sure I was going to die.) We tried exposure therapy, and he upped my Xanax dose. On the day of the flight to Canada, I took one dose in the morning and another 30 minutes before the flight, then kept my mind occupied by playing a casual game for the duration of the flight. It worked really well. The whole trip went smoothly, even though we had to go through Customs.

And it was an amazing cruise. Almost my whole family made it. My sister and her family couldn't come because their kids were too small. My brother left his two kids with their grandparents and was like, "We're going." Guess who else didn't come? Yeah. Marla. After the whole rigamarole. The trip was scheduled during the time that Byron would be in Europe, and she didn't want to leave the country while he was out of the country "just in case." Which I understood, but it was still hard on me. Naturally, that made it harder for her to appreciate the gravity of what I'd managed to do ... but I still expected more of a reaction on her part. All in all, I took three flights without incident this summer. I was feeling really proud of myself—and then Marla's father died. No way could I ask for recognition in the midst of her grief.

That's when I consciously gave up on our marriage, and started waiting for her to tell me that she's done.

Marla says she has no intention of leaving the relationship. She still says, "I love you." But in my mind, it's a very odd and strained relationship at this point. I ask her what she gets out of our marriage and she doesn't have an answer. It sucks, because I really thought I'd found the right person ... but unless some key things change, I don't know how much longer I'll be married.

“

Why do we feel compelled to get married? Marriage, as we know it, is rooted in patriarchal rule, where fathers used to literally give away their daughters, who were their property. I half-jokingly feel that marriage is the special interest that benefits divorce lawyers.

I've had several relationships and two grown children. Now I've been alone for years, and I'm finally okay with it. I go to restaurants and movies by myself, and sometimes people feel sorry for me, and ask if I want to join them. I'm not that far removed from the generation where women used to sign their name as Mrs. Their Husband's Name. I want to enjoy my freedom, but I'm constantly battling this internal dialog with the societal interject that I'd be happier, more fulfilled, whatever, if I were married, and that I am somehow diminished without a mate.

—A. M. (52)
Original Austinite

“

While I am glad to have the right, as a gay man, to marry (and exercised that right myself), I find the whole idea of marriage bizarre and antiquated. My partner and I only married because our lives together necessitate it. We don't wear rings, didn't have a ceremony, and don't refer to ourselves as husbands. The ‘performance’ of marriage is not something either of us have an interest in being a part of.

Marriage is an institution and a bankrupt one at that. There is too much pressure on men and women, boys and girls, to conform to something that is nothing more than a social construct born out of a parochial, religious dogma. Sex before marriage? Please. Who cares?

People should be free to marry as they so choose and I have no ill will against those who choose that path. However, I have deep reservations about the commercialization of marriage and society's more or less blind, uniform approbation of an institution which serves no obvious purpose outside of reifying social, racial, and class divisions.

—Perry (30)
Peace Corps volunteer

KATIE & REIGH

[After Donald Trump was elected president, Katie (25) and her wife Reigh (25) no longer felt safe in the United States. They decided to move to Canada—Reigh's home country—to escape queer and racial persecution. It's been a hard adjustment for Katie, who temporarily lost her sense of self last year ... but they're figuring out their new lives one day at a time.]

2016

Katie and Reigh 'met' via the microblogging platform Tumblr. Devoted fans of the spoken word poet Andrea Gibson, Katie was searching for videos of Andrea's work when she found Reigh's blog, complete with transcriptions of the poet's best-loved performances. "Anyone who loves Andrea Gibson as much as I do is probably a pretty cool person," Katie says, explaining why she started following Reigh on social media. "I went to her blog and I really liked all the things that were going on there. We had all the same interests, so I sent her a message."

Reigh thought Katie's random message was "cool," but that was she "likely a weirdo," so she didn't respond. In fact, she forgot about it entirely until one night when she couldn't sleep and decided to post something "more personal" than her usual shares: "Someone send me a love," she wrote. "I have so much love to give!" Embarrassed, Reigh immediately deleted the post—but not before Katie saw it. She took a chance at messaging Reigh one more time. "Hey, I saw your post. I feel that way as well—SO much love to give." Katie sent the message on what she called her "single-year-versary." (She had been single for a year and that was the benchmark she had given herself to start dating again.)

"I was not ready to start loving someone over the internet," says Reigh, so the women took things slowly. Inspired by Andrea's poem "Asking Too Much" (in which the poet asks a series of questions considered "too much" on a first date), Reigh asked Katie the first question:

> I want you to tell me about every person you've ever been in love with / Tell me why you loved them, / then tell me why they loved you

Katie answered at length, then ended by asking Reigh the next question—and in that way they made it through the whole poem. "We ended up knowing so much about each other," Reigh remembers. "Then I was going home for Christmas, and I'm a very clear person, and my dad was like, 'What's wrong with you? ... You're in love!' And I was like, 'Ew, no. With who?' and he said, 'I'm going to find out who.'" By that point, Reigh and Katie were texting and emailing but had not yet talked or video-chatted. Later that night, Reigh's dad saw her texting and said: "Her. That girl. You're in love with her." Reigh realized it was true, but that she didn't even know Katie's name!

"She knew my parents' names and my deepest secrets," Katie clarifies. "The biggest lies I'd ever told anyone. The worst thought I'd ever had about my best friend. But we'd never exchanged real names."

"It felt like I could tell this person anything," adds Reigh. "She was going to school in Michigan; I lived in Canada. I was never going to meet her, so it was safe."

That night, Reigh texted Katie: "By the way ... what's your name?" Three days later, the social ice broken, they started sending pictures. At first the photos were fairly anonymous: a shot of Reigh's new rib tattoo, for example, cropped to cut out her face.

"She was flirting with me," says Katie. "It was probably the best way to meet someone. I knew everything I loved about her before I even knew what she looked like." Still, the pair didn't plan on meeting—and "definitely" never foresaw their long-distance, cross-country relationship.

On Christmas evening 2012, Katie and Reigh agreed to Skype for the first time. Reigh was 19. Katie had just turned 20. "There was a lot of blushing," Katie recalls. "A lot of blushing," Reigh echoes. "And giggling. I was drinking wine and Katie was like, 'Oh, I'll have a glass of wine with you!' Which I later found out was pomegranate juice because she was just so nervous."

"I was nervous and I didn't want to say anything stupid while drunk. I wanted to be so present. In retrospect I should've drank, because the feelings I had upon hearing Reigh's voice for the first time were unreal. I didn't know she had so many freckles until I saw her in person. I fell in love with every one of them."

"Same," says Reigh. "I thought I'd been in love before, but it hadn't been like it was with Katie. So much giddiness and excitement. Also sadness, because it was never going to happen." Neither student could afford to visit the other, and even if they could, they had different academic schedules. Their spring breaks didn't align. "But then I faked a rugby injury to skip a tournament in Vegas, and I used the flight credit to visit Katie in Michigan instead." That was February

2013—also known as "the best day" of Katie's life.

It almost didn't happen. A huge snowstorm hit Toronto, and Reigh's flight got canceled at the last minute. Her only alternative was to board a train to Windsor, Canada, just across the border from Detroit. Katie (who had just come down with the stomach flu!) drove from Kalamazoo to Detroit and tried to cross into Canada. "Imagine explaining your situation to a border control agent in the amount of time they give you," she says. "Gay marriage wasn't legal yet, so I said, 'I'm going to pick up my friend from the train station.'" When the agent asked how they knew each other, Katie gave the first answer that came to mind: "We met at band camp a couple of years ago."

"We had to lie at the border," Reigh notes, "several times. But when I saw her in that train station ... I ran to her, and held her face so close to mine that I could barely even see her. It didn't matter that she had the flu and felt like shit. I hadn't slept or eaten either, but it was perfect."

"Then she met my parents two hours later," laughs Katie.

"Yup, that was horrible."

Hugging Reigh: "She's a trooper."

"Nah, they were nice to me. Mostly. I think they were just relieved to see I was a real person and not a serial killer."

After their first successful visit, and with their parents' blessings, Katie flew to see Reigh in March. Reigh would come back to the States one more time that same month. Then in May 2013, Reigh finished her school year and flew to Kalamazoo for a week. Katie still had a month left in her semester. At the airport, Katie said, "I really don't want you to leave!"

"I really don't want to leave, either," Reigh sighed.

"Then don't?"

"Okay!"

Reigh ended up staying until Katie's school year ended. She lived in Katie's off-campus house with her, which didn't thrill Katie's 7 roommates. "Bad call on all the parts," says Katie, "but I still wouldn't change it. We were young and in love."

Near the end of that summer, Katie left for a six-month study abroad program in India. The ladies still Skyped but couldn't visit each other, amounting to an agonizing autumn. When Katie got back, she and Reigh took a Christmas trip to Nicaragua. There, the couple got engaged—twice.

As Reigh describes it, "Nicaragua was hard because it was our first time traveling together, and while I'd been sitting at home bored for six months, Katie had already been traveling for six months, so she was tired. We stayed in this treehouse hostel, a 45-minute hike up the mountain in 100-degree heat. Every day I wanted to climb volcanoes and she was like, 'I just want to sit down.'"

Not to mention that Katie was carrying a heavy bottle of champagne in her backpack, just waiting for the right moment to propose. She'd bought a ring for Reigh in India and was planning to surprise her.

What Katie didn't know was that Reigh had also bought a ring, and it was burning a hole in her pocket. One evening Reigh suggested that they walk out on the nearby suspension bridge overlooking the sunset. She had read somewhere that attraction levels go up on suspension bridges because of the fear element. "I thought: *I can't lose if I do it on this bridge. She'll think I'm a total catch!*" In the dying light on the middle of the bridge, Reigh popped the question and Katie said "Yes."

"I was a little mad because I wanted to go first," Katie smiles. "But I forgave you, since it was so nice. Then we opened our very warm champagne and drank from our Nalgene bottles."

Katie still wanted her turn to propose, so she picked the day of their one-year dating anniversary. As it happened, they were in downtown León that day—a day "so hot," says Reigh, "that I took a nap and almost drowned in my own drool." The heat made the women grumpy with one another; they couldn't decide how to spend the day and bickered a bunch. For dinner, Reigh suggested they go to El Carnívoro, a restaurant known for its meat preparation. Reigh was a vegetarian at the time, but wanted Katie to have her favorite dish: beef carpaccio. At the restaurant, things continued to go awry. Reigh ordered a fancy cocktail that the bartender was supposed to light on fire, but instead "he just poured gasoline on it. He was supposed to light the liquor, but instead he used gas, so then I drank some gas, and then because I'm not a wasteful person, I drank the whole thing."

By the time they got back to the hotel, Reigh was sick and Katie thought the whole anniversary had been miserable. *Even so*, she thought, *Reigh is still the person that I want to do every single day of my life with ... including and especially the worst days. Now is the time*. She called Reigh out to the little balcony attached to their room, and presented her with a carved stone box that she'd bought at the Taj Mahal in India. Getting down on one knee, she said, "I can't build you a monument to my love like the Taj Mahal; this is as close as I can get." The night air was thick with the scent of guava trees. "Whenever we smell guava," Katie says, "it brings back happy memories for us."

The following day, their grumpiness had dissipated and they passed the rest of the trip in style. They hit up a dance club on New Years Eve ("and ate the best tacos we've ever had," adds Reigh), and Reigh even got to climb her active volcano. "You could look down into it at the lava," she says. "Which was awesome but then Katie started leaning too far over and I was like, 'We've been engaged for a day, please don't die.'"

When they returned to the States, Reigh was supposed to head back to Canada right away; her visitor's visa was set to expire. The couple had talked about doing six months in Canada, six months in the States ad infinitum, but realized such a plan would not be conducive to sustaining school, jobs, or general happiness. "Fuck it, let's just get married and you can live here," Katie said. While they'd envisioned a five-year engagement, they got married five months later, in May 2014. Reigh stayed in the States illegally all that time, completing her classes online while living with Katie's roommates.

One unexpected benefit of becoming engaged was being able to call each other "fiancée." Although Reigh and Katie say they haven't experienced "a lot" of queer discrimination, the word "fiancée" (when spoken aloud) sounds the same as the word "fiancé." Instead of referring to her "girlfriend," Katie could talk about her fiancée Reigh and people assumed she meant a man ("Ray"). "It was especially important while we were traveling in Nicaragua," Katie says, "and weren't completely sure about their okayness with our queerness. So I'd say 'my fiancée' and the look on their face was like, *Oh, congratulations, young straight couple!* Then Reigh would walk up and all of a sudden we weren't being offered free room service anymore."

"It's nothing terrible," allows Reigh, "and really I'd say we've been a lot luckier than we would've been at any other time in recent history. Honestly, the worst incident I think we've had was 2 weeks ago now."

In November 2016, Katie and Reigh signed up to participate in a 5K Fun Run in Round Rock. Katie's not a big runner so she and Reigh walked most of the race, holding hands. Reigh wanted to run across the finish line, so she went ahead of Katie, telling her, "I'll meet you there." As soon as Reigh took off, four preteen girls who had been walking in front of the couple turned around, linked hands, and formed a human 'wall.' They deliberately blocked Katie's path while shouting "She's a lesbian! Build that wall!"

Says Katie: "It was terrifying, especially because my parents and I had gotten in a fight just a few days before. My dad was like, 'If you're so afraid about what's going to happen post-election, why are you going out and doing things? Why are you going to the run on Saturday?' 'Because I'm not going to stop living my life or stop having fun,' I told him. 'I'm allowed to feel afraid even if I want to go do stuff.' Really, the whole incident was just a shame. They were children: 10 or 12 years old. They learn that hate from school and from their parents."

Reigh and Katie experienced similar treatment in Ann Arbor, a Michigan city often compared to Austin for its "liberal, progressive mindset." One day the women were walking down the street, holding hands, and they kissed at the corner. A passerby lewdly asked, "Can you do that again?" Other than that, though, they've found society at large to be "fairly accepting," and it helps that their parents feel similarly. As Katie says, "They're not the most homophobic people in the world. I wasn't kicked out of the house when I came out in high school. Reigh's family is more religious, so there's that, but they also seem to realize there are bigger issues in the world."

Reigh: "When I came out, it wasn't like 'We accept you.' It was more like, 'I'm sure Jesus cares more about starving children than your gayness.'"

When the couple got married (in a courthouse in Windsor), none of their family members attended except for Katie's sister. That was less a commentary on their support, though, and more because the women gave them four days' notice. "We thought we were being considerate by saying, 'We know it's short notice, so we don't expect you to be there, though we'd love it if you could make it,'" explains Katie. "Instead, they took it as a dis-invitation and didn't come."

"Luckily," says Reigh, "everyone got past that, and later Katie's parents threw us a small party in Austin. They gave us a wedding book and a notepad and champagne glasses with our names on them." Katie and Reigh started using the notepad to leave each other love notes. Over the past year, they've amassed a "pretty big stack" of love notes—a practice they hope to continue for 70 more years.

About six months after they were legally married, Reigh filed for permanent residence. The following May (of 2015), she met with an immigration officer who helped smooth the way for this 'illegal immigrant.' "It was this weird thing," recalls Reigh, "where I wasn't allowed to be in the country (because she had overstayed her visa), but I couldn't file for residency if I was outside of the country, either." To 'prove' their relationship, the women were interviewed separately, and asked to provide documentation like a joint Costco card and dual gym membership. While the immigration officer did his thing, Reigh kept living with Katie in Kalamazoo. At 21, Katie had one more year of college. School was slower-going for Reigh, who could only take so many online classes at a time.

Once Katie graduated in June 2015 (and Reigh's green card had been granted), the couple moved to Austin, Texas. "We made a spreadsheet of 15 cities with 20 must-haves," says Katie. "Things like 'A city that's big but not New York or LA-big.' Bike lanes. Nature trails. Good weather. A rugby team for Reigh. Poutine." Austin was #4 or #5 on that list, but it had one thing going for it that no other city did: Katie's parents lived there, and if they were going to move some place new, it would help to have a support system. "Especially parents who say, 'Let us take you to dinner because you just zapped all your funds moving here.'"

"Her parents were also willing to front the downpayment for our condo if we moved to Austin," notes Reigh. "The house was in their name, but we paid the mortgage; it was the sensible thing to do." So they took their two cats and hit the road.

In Austin, Reigh found work first at the Humane Society. A couple weeks later, Katie took a part-time nonprofit position, and supplemented her income by serving as her mom's executive assistant. They lived on "fairly meager" means, but were otherwise quite happy (though in Reigh's opinion, there aren't enough people of color in Austin). The plan was to stay in Texas 3-5 years, then maybe move again to start a family of their own.

But then Donald Trump took office, and Reigh's and Katie's reactions were violent. As Reigh puts it: "Trump doesn't scare me, but the hate he engenders does. Now people are being vocal about their hate—like it's 'safe' to be sexist, homophobic, and racist because the president-elect is."

"That's how you end up with a string of 12-year-old girls linking arms and saying, 'Build the wall!'" adds Katie. "I'm like, 'That's not even what the wall is for!' The scary thing is that they're saying it when they don't even know what it means."

Katie's parents responded to their daughter's fears with condescension, which both Reigh and Katie say they understand. "They're a middle-aged, straight, white, very wealthy couple. They have none of the issues we have, which is hard for them. Their thinking is, 'Just don't hold hands in public then. Don't put yourself in a place where you won't be safe.' It's the same kind of victim-blaming that happens with sexual assault survivors," Katie says.

Trump's election also followed on the heels of several racially-motivated police shootings in Summer 2016—a tragedy especially concerning to Reigh. She came home from work one day and said to her wife: "I don't want to live here anymore." It was a hard pill for Katie, who was heavily invested in diversity and inclusion advocacy in Austin, to swallow, "but Reigh's safety and well-being is more important than all that," she says. "I don't want her to live in fear. It's terrifying to me that she might get pulled over one day for a simple traffic violation and that might be the last time that I ever see her. It's something that black Americans and other people live with everyday, but we can't accept that as our reality."

So the women announced their decision to move. To Canada.

The news did not go over well with Katie's family. They're conservative, and they feared that Katie and Reigh would "run off and never talk to them again." "Slow down," they told their daughter and daughter-in-law. "Save up. Bureaucracy moves slowly. Nothing's going to happen for 2-3 years."

"They don't realize that the bureaucracy is not what we are scared of," comments Katie.

Katie's parents also resented being saddled with the couple's condo, and so retaliated with an immediate financial disownment. "We want all our money back, right now," they said, expecting Katie and Reigh to reproduce the condo downpayment on the spot.

"I naively thought the downpayment had been a gift," Katie says. "My parents paid for my sister's big wedding. Since we didn't have a wedding, I thought the downpayment was a gift-in-kind. I was too shy to say that, though—so I took out a loan to pay them back."

The weeks leading up to Thanksgiving were fraught with family tension. Katie and Reigh thought about skipping the family dinner, but decided to go at the last minute. Katie's dad especially appreciated what he interpreted as a "goodwill gesture" that helped to heal some hurt feelings before the ladies leave the country. Their scheduled date of departure is December 19, 2016.

On her way to a holiday party a few weeks ago, Reigh stopped at a gas station to buy some alcohol. The attendant asked for her ID, so Reigh gave him her green card. She assumed he was an immigrant himself, because he seemed familiar with it. Handing it back, he warned Reigh, "You know, this is going to expire soon. You should have reapplied already. It's not safe here if your green card expires." She says she was "well aware" that it was close to expiring, but that she hadn't bothered reapplying since she knew they were leaving the country. "It was alarming to see how scared he was for me, though," she comments. His reaction reinforced her belief that leaving the country is the best idea.

It will be much easier for Katie to immigrate to Canada. "Canada has a very low population," says Reigh. "Almost one-tenth the size of the States—so they want immigrants. There's also less xenophobia. It'll just be a waiting game: a couple years and a couple hundred dollars."

For Reigh, it will be a homecoming. The couple plans to live with Reigh's parents and siblings who still live at home for the first year, while they save money. Reigh anticipates it will be "uncomfortable. We're moving into a madhouse. But it's a better country for us. Gay marriage has been legal in Canada since 2005, and Prime Minister Trudeau is awesome, for the most part."

Katie: "And gun laws. I won't have to be afraid (I hope) of walking down the street there, holding hands with the woman I love."

Reigh: "I'm looking forward to not feeling like I'm the only person of color."

Katie: "I expect it will be colder in Canada, but I lived in Michigan for 23 years, so I'll be ready!"

Reigh & Katie

2017

[At time of writing, Reigh and Katie have lived in Canada for ten days shy of one year. They live with Reigh's parents, her 22-year-old brother, her 26-year-old sister, and her sister's partner and two kids. The couple has been back to the U.S. four times for friends' weddings and to visit Katie's family. Katie just received her Canadian work permit; she is still waiting to gain permanent residency status.]

Almost a year in, Reigh maintains that moving to Canada remains the best choice that she and Katie could have made, but that "we probably could have been less hasty. If we'd stayed in Texas longer to save up more money, or waited for Trump to actually deport me, maybe we could have afforded our own place." As things stand, they share one house with nine people and four animals. "It's a full house, and a little unfair to Katie," admits Reigh. "I would not sign up to live with her family for a year."

Next month, Reigh's stepbrother and his partner are set to move out of the backyard pool house, and the ladies plan to move in for a bit more privacy. Right now, a thin door and thinner floors separate them in the basement from the rest of the family above. One bright spot for both women this year was the birth of their newest nephew, Bryson—Reigh's sister's kid. Having an infant around has been a "big change" (in a good way). Says Katie: "We really needed some reprieve from the tension that has been in the house, and he brought a lot of joy."

Setting them back financially was the fact that, until a month ago, Katie wasn't able to work. It took eight months for her work permit to clear, meaning the couple had to rely on Reigh's income alone. (She's an office manager for a social services nonprofit.) Just recently, Katie got hired to run the University of Alberta's gender and sexuality center. She facilitates meetups and develops resources for LGBTQ students and allies, and feels grateful that both she and Reigh are at last working in fields they like.

"It's been the hardest year of our relationship yet," Katie says. "We lived alone for a year and a half; living with so many other people now is challenging. Also, because I wasn't working, I felt like I wasn't contributing. My life didn't have a clear meaning. At any point, I could have left and gone back to Austin and said, 'We're just gonna wait it out until things are more settled.' But I'm still here.

"Something that I really admire about Reigh," she continues, "is that she doesn't let me hold a grudge against her for longer than an hour. On really hard days, or even really hard weeks, she's always trying to figure out a way for us to get through it together. So, it's been one of our hardest years, but it's also been one of our best."

Reigh "never felt that Katie wasn't carrying her weight when she couldn't work. But it didn't matter," she claims, "because Katie felt that way. I wasn't doing enough to assuage her feelings of guilt. What I have to understand is that just because I think watching hockey for six hours with my family is really fun, doesn't mean that Katie's not in hell. I try to be sensitive to her needs. Most of the time when we get upset with each other, it's not even about us. It's all these external factors: work (or lack thereof); family; living in cramped quarters."

Katie describes how she and Reigh were both "really grumpy" last night. They couldn't agree on a movie to watch and were taking it out on each other. Reigh asked, "Do you want to say three things we like about each other until we don't get mad at each other anymore?" As soon as she suggested that, Katie was "already smiling and mad at myself for being so weak."

Both women feel like their mental health has suffered since moving to Canada. Katie didn't qualify for Canadian health coverage until July, so she hasn't been to see a doctor yet. She still Skypes weekly with her therapist in Austin, who is helping her to process events from her childhood and adolescence that at age 25 continue to plague her.

A relatively new demon for Katie is body image issues. "Because we weren't able to afford nutritious food when I wasn't working," she explains, "we ate fast food every day, and that does bad things to your body. I don't think we're 'healthy' people right now in any sense of the word." For a while the couple tried sharing meals with Reigh's family, but that quickly worked against them. "When my parents buy a meal," says Reigh, "they're buying everyone a meal. So that means when we buy a meal, we have to buy everyone a meal. It's just not feasible for us to feed nine people, so now we buy our own food, and we buy what we can afford—which is junk."

Desperate to get away and "breathe" for a minute, the ladies retreated to the mountains for their wedding anniversary in May. They live about four hours from the Canadian Rockies, which Katie says are "exceptional." By their own admission, they couldn't afford it but went anyway, renting "a nice room with a bathtub in a nice hotel"—the bathtub being Katie's only "must-have criteria." Together, they went on hikes, saw mountain sheep, and felt largely restored to themselves. "But then we got in a huge fight (about money) on the way back," Reigh sighs. "It was a really awkward four-hour drive."

They got to go back to the mountains the following month, for an extended family vacation. It would be the first time that Reigh's and Katie's parents met. "It was so awkward I thought I was gonna die," shares Reigh. "I never relaxed the whole time," agrees Katie. Katie was "positive" that her parents would say something "pretentious" and alienate Reigh's family. But they didn't. Everyone got along. Katie's mom was particularly "warm and hospitable," welcoming Reigh's family to the cabin they'd rented for the week. In retrospect, the ladies didn't know why it'd taken so long for them to meet. "Everyone thought we were embarrassed of everyone else, but for weeks after that visit, every time we talked to either set of parents, they'd be like, 'Oh, your parents are so lovely.'"

In between there, Katie actually won a trip to Japan! She entered a contest on Twitter that required entrants to argue in 140 words why they should be picked to explore gay culture in Tokyo. Katie wrote about working in UA's gender and diversity center. "We're such an international school, and it would be helpful to understand a different cultural perspective," she wrote. She and 24 others received a six-day, five-night all-expenses-paid trip to the city "Where Old Meets New." Of course she brought Reigh along with her; how could they pass up a buy-one, get-one trip of a lifetime? They decided to worry about paying for it later.

In Japan, Katie's only obligation as a contest winner was to go out with the other winners to a gay bar on the first night and hear a local artist discuss the impact of manga on queer culture. The whole trip was "such a wild experience," Katie's still wrapping her head around it. Reigh "loved" Japan; she expected to hate it. She thought there'd be too many people, and that the language barrier would leave her confused and overwhelmed. "My dream life is to live on an island where it's just me, and like, a cow," she laughs. "But Tokyo was amazing. Everyone was so respectful and quiet, and the food was so efficient. We ordered on an iPad and our meals came to our seat on a conveyor belt."

Steve Jobs once said that "Coming back to America was, for me, much more of a culture shock than going to India." Katie might agree with that sentiment. While there were certainly new things to take in in Japan, she returned to a country that she's struggling to make her own, and which has required its own breed of adaptation. "Canadians pronounce some words differently," she says. "Like pasta. Americans say pah-stuh. Canadians say pay-stuh." Canadian food is better quality, but more expensive. The exchange rate isn't favorable, making American loan repayment "a bitch." Moose and coyote wander into their edge-of-the-prairie backyard. People are "generally friendlier," she says, and every neighborhood has a free community ice rink instead of a swimming pool.

As Katie continues 'settling in,' Reigh think it's high time for 2017 to end already. "We need a new year," she says. "This year was shit; it's nice that the calendar allows you to be like, 'Okay! Starting over.' Obviously, it's not quite as easy as all that, but I'm glad that as the year wraps up, we can just tuck it away, blame Trump, and move on."

In 2018, Reigh (who has yet to finish college) plans to quit her job and go back to school full-time. Even though doing so would leave them financially strapped again, Katie supports the idea. "It would give you more opportunity to do what you want to do," she says softly to her wife, "which will make you happier, which will make me happier, which will make it a better year."

Katie would like to go back to India and see the students she taught there, all of whom will age out of the school this year. "If we are not reckless with our finances and instead actually plan a trip, we could pull it off and have a really good time there."

Further down the road, the future looks hazy. They don't know if they'll try to foster, adopt, or have kids of their own, or if being the "cool aunts" will prove enough for them. They definitely want to keep traveling—"Maybe we'll buy an island in Nicaragua," Reigh says.

One thing is certain: they have their youth going for them. Katie: "We got married so young, that our 30-year anniversary will be when we're 50. It seems fun." She pauses, reflecting. "I'd like to see you with white hair, babe. I think you'd look great."

"Yeah," adds Reigh. "We get extra time. We'll be the really annoying people causing a ruckus in the nursing home!"

“

The one practical reason to get married is that it may encourage people to work through their problems, since divorce is such a pain in the ass. If it wasn't for marriage, you could pick up and leave, no consequences.

I've been married twice, and I won't do it again. My first wife gets 32% of my salary in alimony payments—and she works and has her own income! We were married for 28 years, but that's hardly fair.

Our kids were 22 and 14 when we divorced. Two years later, I asked my younger daughter how the divorce had affected her. She said, "Oh, my friends would come over and be like 'What's with your parents?'" It was obvious to everyone, even our kids and their friends, that we had a loveless marriage. Thus our divorce made sense to them.

Nevertheless, researchers say that both sexes live longer if they're married. Something about less stress, and less social isolation. I guess we'll see.

—Mike (59)
Bio-pharmaceutical engineer

[*from* "A Site to Help Get Wedding Bells Ringing and Ringing and Ringing"]

In 2014, Azad Chaiwala (now 33) founded SecondWife.com, a site which matches married Muslim men with single Muslim women interested in sharing a spouse. He followed up this venture in late 2016 with Polygamy.com—same concept, but open to anyone, not just Muslims.

According to Mr. Chaiwala, his sites offer "a pro-family antidote to promiscuity, prostitution, divorce, and broken homes."

"I am saying, 'Marry two or three, and be loyal to them.'"

—*The New York Times* (20 September 2016)

SHEILA & RAJ

[Sheila (51) is a businesswoman and mom in North Houston. She was born in India, but immigrated with her parents to California in early childhood. There she met Raj (52), the father of her kids and the perfectly imperfect love of her life. "Marriage," she says, "is a commitment to constant growth in union with another human being."]

2016

My husband's name is Rajesh, but everyone calls him Raj. Raj's sister Sona is the one who introduced us, after she and I met at an engagement party for a mutual friend. She listened to me describe my ideal man—tall, dark, and handsome; born in India, but raised in the States; with at least a master's degree—and said, "You have to meet my brother! You two are perfect for each other!" She and Raj were taking a group ski trip the following month in Nevada, and she invited me to join them.

"Thanks, but no thanks," I said, hoping to politely head her off. My parents had been setting me up with Indian men left and right, many of them duds. The last thing I wanted was to be stuck in the mountains with someone who would propose as soon as he saw me. (Yes, this happened. It's called introduced dating. Your parents and friends circulate a bio-sheet with your photo, stats, and accomplishments, and men reply with marriage proposals. My parents came with me on many face-to-face 'dates.' It was a series of comedic meetings.)

What nobody knew was that secretly I was in an eight-year relationship with a Caucasian guy. Tony. He'd been my hush-hush high school sweetheart, and then we'd gone to college together at UCLA. I never told anyone about him because I was afraid of disappointing my parents and of being ostracized from the Indian community. While my mom and dad said over and over, "You're done with school. You need to get married," I sat with Tony and wished that everything was different. When I finally found the courage to talk to my parents about our relationship, I was surprised that after their initial disappointment, they gave me the permission to do what made me happy. But back then I didn't believe I deserved my own happiness. Not when everyone around me had sacrificed so much for it.

So I left Tony and went to India with my parents and let them play matchmaker. They introduced me to fat men and short men and kind men and fair men and 'good Punjabi men' and men with whom I couldn't communicate because we had nothing to say to each other. Some of them looked really great on paper, but didn't hold up in person. I was cautious and skeptical because I'd heard horror stories about Indian men who married American women for the green card, only to enter the States and run off with the first blonde they saw. I was scared because having been with Tony, I knew what happy felt like—and I wasn't sure I'd get that if I 'settled.'

*

I never went to Nevada; Nevada came to me. After Raj, his sister, and their friends spent a long weekend skiing, Sona called and asked if we could all meet for dinner. "7:00 tonight," she said, naming a restaurant in Los Angeles. I lived an hour away in Orange County. It was Sunday, the weather was bad, and I had work the next day. (I was a physical therapist then.) But I grudgingly agreed.

I drove though torrential rain to get there, and ten minutes late, was the first to arrive. Two hours later, they had yet to show—so I left. This was the early '90s. We didn't have cell phones. As far as I knew, I'd been stood up. Almost as soon as I walked back in the door, the house phone rang. It was Sona, wondering where I was. "Where am I? I came home! You're three hours late!" I exploded.

"Yes," she admitted, "but you've got to come back. Raj's such a great guy. I would love for you to meet him. Please."

For reasons unknown to me, I got back in the car and drove back to Los Angeles at 10:00 p.m. on a Sunday night. And I am happy to report that it was love at first sight. Raj and I were mesmerized by each other. Our dinner went until 3:00 in the morning. Then I went back to Orange County and he went back to Houston, Texas. I figured that was it. "He's great," I said, when my family asked how it had gone. "He's handsome and funny and a competent engineer. But he lives in Houston. It's not worth it." I left it at that.

Then Raj sent me a birthday gift in February. We started talking on the phone every day, and every few weeks one of us would fly to see the other for a weekend. Six months later, we got engaged. Six months after that we were married.

Our wedding was magical. A fairytale. I wanted

to be the princess at my wedding and I was. Over 500 people attended a party that lasted for days—because that's how Indians are and because that's what I wanted. We had one traditional wedding, with no meat or alcohol, and another, larger reception with meat, booze, and dancing. We danced to *A Whole New World* from Aladdin and I was whisked into this la-la land where I wasn't even conscious of having 1000 eyes on me. When I think of that moment, I remember why I'm still living. No matter how angry I get at Raj sometimes, or how sick I would get in the years to come.

My parents loved Raj, but more than anything they were relieved. At 28, I was pushing the envelope of 'old age.' I was relieved, too. I wanted to be married, but I didn't want to settle—and with Raj, I didn't have to. Divorce was a cultural taboo. You married for life. I saw a lot of women my age settle, and then they were stuck. They didn't try to make their marriages work. Like candy, they wanted divorce because it was something they couldn't have. In the last few years, I've developed a very deep understanding of what choice means. When you choose to be with somebody, even though it's difficult, you choose something other than *what has to be*. In Raj, I found someone I could choose and re-choose every day of my life.

It was a lucky thing, too, because just after we got married, my mom was diagnosed with stage 4 ovarian cancer and I spent almost the whole first year of our marriage taking care of her. Raj stayed in Texas, building a custom home for us, but he visited as often as he could and supported me 100%. Not a day went by that I didn't think, "Man, did I chose a good guy." Raj didn't even know my family that well, but he just dove in with two feet and his whole heart.

*

I'm fascinated by this concept of 'modern' marriage. A lot of people choose not to get married these days. Is that modern marriage? I know couples who have been together for 15 years. Why are they still together? "Because we don't have to be," they tell me. "Because we choose to be." Is that modern marriage? Other people insist that no one stays committed anymore. That you have to want to stay in your marriage, and that's hard work—'too' hard, given a society that chases instant gratification. So is that the hallmark of modern marriage?

I was thinking about this when I woke up on the morning of my 24th wedding anniversary. My marriage hasn't always been easy, but it's gotten easier in the past couple years as I've redefined what I want from it. To me, a 'modern' marriage is one where you commit to constant growth in union with another human being. Everyone experiences challenges where they think, "This sucks. I don't feel respected. I don't feel appreciated." Those moments are opportunities to grow, to choose to stay in it and to sit with the discomfort—which is probably the hardest thing I've ever done besides childbirth. It's finding understanding between two very strong human beings. I think so many people are getting divorced just because it's tough. But life is an inner job. This partner of mine is a master teacher, so why would I leave him? He's going to give me the most difficult, challenging opportunities to become a better person. He's teaching me to have a voice, to listen better, and to be more accepting—of myself and others.

Like attracts like, no doubt; but in a solid marriage, our partners hold the mirror for us. They show us what needs healing internally, and we attract people capable of helping us heal. The things that we're here to develop, the other person brings to the table so we can learn. Raj's very intellectual and I'm very emotional. Those aren't good or bad things; they're complementary qualities. It means that he thinks about it and I feel it. I tend to be more extroverted, he tends to be more private. We need that—I learn from him what I can hold inside myself, and I teach him how to be more candid. His low self-esteem shows up as overconfidence. Mine shows up as self-effacement. We're healing that in each other.

When you resist the growing pains (because they hurt!), you merely send them somewhere else in your body. I believe very firmly that our thoughts and beliefs and actions settle into our physical body, where they manifest as a vibrant, healthy, flowing body, or a stagnant, diseased body. If you feel like there's no way out, your body creates ways for you to exit. Many years ago now, I was overwhelmed and didn't know what I wanted. My father, my last living relative, had just died, and I was put in charge of his estate in California. I was living in Houston, trying to raise two children, be a supportive wife, and also run a business for which I never had enough time. My cancer diagnosis didn't happen by chance. I wanted out of my life. The message I was giving my body was "I can't do it all," so my body said, "Okay, don't. Just let go."

Modern marriage is a place of choice and freedom. You can choose to leave or you can choose to grow through it, sore muscles (and sore ego!) and all. It's like anything—if you give the child no choice, they'll rebel; but if you give them freedom, they might choose exactly what you wanted them to choose.

*

I had zero examples of a 'good' marriage growing up. At the same time that I didn't want to disappoint my parents in my choice of mate, I also knew that I didn't want what they had. Mom and Dad grew up next-door neighbors. My mother and my dad's sister were best friends, so they saw each other all the time. So it wasn't an arranged marriage, but it wasn't love, either. It was familiar. By the time they started having kids, they quarreled all the time—usually about us. I was afraid of that arguing, and of being miserable every day of my life. What I try to teach my children now (we have a 20-year-old boy and an 18-year-old girl) is that if you're going to live under the same roof as somebody, you have to maintain healthy communication as a core requirement. Otherwise, forget it. Passion is great: it can last an entire marriage, but it's like a roller coaster. It can feel really good, then really horrible. I want that steady state of amazement every day.

The same went for my aunts and uncles. They put on their game faces in public, smiling their ways through social settings regardless of what was happening at home. No one taught me what healthy marriage was because we didn't talk about it. You didn't speak up about mistreatment or speak out about gender roles or say anything at all about women's liberation. 'Strong' men were desired and 'soft' men were derided and women took care of the kids and the home.

Now as women pursue education and careers and also still raise families, they've just added more roles without redistributing responsibility, increasing stress and fueling resentment. We're finally at a place where we can speak up and the question we're asking is: "Is this really the way of life?" I'm educated, I worked, I climbed the corporate ladder, but I never connected with the fiery energy of the feminist movement. I lost myself trying to find myself—and in trying to be everything to everyone. Men are equally lost today. Biologically programmed to be the warrior, the hunter, the supporter, and the protector, they're losing those roles to women, and they're still not supposed to show their emotions. Women are coming into their power but men aren't being encouraged to develop their emotional centers. We're forgetting that before we're women, we're human. Before they're men, they're human. We're all just human at the core.

So rather than a women's liberation movement, we need a human liberation movement: individual choice and balanced marriages and a doing away with 'right' and 'wrong.' There are some things that we can't fight nature on: only women can bear and nurse children, for example. Meaning that while husbands and wives might find an equal playing ground, mothers and fathers still can't. It doesn't mean he can't be a stay-at-home-dad, but Mom still has to pump, so that dynamic requires a little more thought and conscious negotiation.

I always wanted to be a mom, and I'm so grateful for the opportunity. What I love the most is that I've woken up to what it is to be a real mom. One who gets to show my humanness—which I've just started doing, because before I was Supermom. Everything was always perfect. They made it to every activity, they were always dressed well, the house was always clean, I always organized playdates, they ate incredibly healthy diets. But now I think a real mom is not Supermom but Human-Mom. Only recently have I had the privilege of modeling who that is, and I get to share my flaws and mistakes. It's not like "Here's what you should do," but "Here's where I made my mistakes, and now I'm giving you all the tools to choose." It's a sharp departure from the strict way in which I was raised.

25 years ago, I was the oldest bachclorette in my Indian immigrant community, and there were so few Indian men available who'd been raised in the United States. In contrast, all of my daughter's friends were, like her, born and raised here—so she has her pick of the litter. It's not important to us, though, that she or our son marry within the Indian culture. We've never said anything about who they can be with, just that, "You've got to be happy. Whatever that is to you, you have to find that." I'm probably more open than my husband in general because I know what it's like to hide who you're dating, but he supports our children's choices regardless.

*

The reason so much has changed for Raj's and my relationship in the last couple years is that the kids are growing older. They're moving out of the house. For the first time since our son was born, we have time to focus on us. It's finally not about survival anymore, like it was for such a long time. Between my parents dying, helping to raise my siblings after they died, my brother's hip injury, our son getting deathly ill when he was very young, and then my cancer, it was all so touch-and-go. Now our goals, which were once so mired in kids and work, are about play and travel and financial freedom. Enjoying each other, and remembering why we got together in the first place. We're really excited about this phase. We've raised two beautiful children, and it's our time again.

It's a journey, marriage. All of this is a journey. Marriage, life—it's not about the 'quick fix.' It's about owning it. I don't know anyone else who would have stood by my side through everything that life threw at us the way that my husband did and continues to do. That's real love, I think: when we can see the 'ouch' and see the love in it. When we can see the not-so-good and see the love in it. I was having an argument with Raj the other day, and I'm really trying to live from this place of 'What am I learning and what am I preaching?' so I realized I had to go kiss him. I had to put my ego aside and remember that hurt people hurt people. Here's what he needed to know: that he is valued, respected, and loved. Is it easy? Not always. But is it worth it? Absolutely and always.

2017

Oh my gosh. I feel more grateful today than I did a year ago. Raj and I have had some huge relational shifts. I am seeing in him what I was incapable of seeing through the eyes of pride. My pride was in the way. It showed up as defensiveness, and trying to prove myself right all the time. My husband wasn't doing that to me; he was holding the mirror for me. Now I feel that I see his essence—who he is—a lot more clearly. We've practiced introspection individually but also as a couple, and I am more grateful than ever to have a man who loves me more than I could ever know. I didn't know. I didn't see it. I didn't appreciate it. Today I'm saying, "Thank you."

Whether you're legally married or in a relationship with a committed partner, the idea is the same. You're declaring to the world that you enjoy this human being, that you've chosen to spend your life walking beside them, and that you recognize that life isn't just about the playful, wonderful things, but about learning difficult lessons together, in the most beautiful and loving way possible. The motto that Raj and I have is: *Do I choose to be right or do I choose to be happy?* Every day I become more committed to being happy and not right. Because being right means we'll fight to the end. So instead I just share what I'm feeling ... and when it's just put out there like, "Here's an honest feeling I'm having; I don't know what it means or whether it's right ... " then all of a sudden there's nothing to argue about. You can't argue over the way somebody feels.

It's such a simple concept, but it doesn't feel simple because we're programmed to think that everything has to be proven. After my bout with cancer, I was trying to prove to the world that I'd healed myself, and that self-healing is possible. But what's actually important is that I'm well, and what's less important is showing the world why and how.

We faced spiritual, emotional, and physical challenges this past year—a little bit of everything that could go wrong. When I say "challenges," I really mean opportunities for both Raj and I to stop and say, "Okay, we've done so much work together, shared so much life together, raised two beautiful kids together; what are we being called to evolve in our relationship now?" We had to slow down and take time, and this was a good year to take it. Marriage requires constant time. If you ever just say, "Oh, we're good," and keep rolling without ever stopping and acknowledging each other, there can be no evolution. And where there's no evolution, there's stagnation. So 2017 was a year that we chose, for many reasons, to take time to see what was next for us.

I think that's why a lot of relationships falter; the couple (as a unit) fails to change along with the individuals (who are constantly evolving), so then they fall apart. Rather than seeing the issues in the marriage as a 'problem,' if you could instead recognize that the issues are arising because the human beings in the relationship are changing, then as we change, we could also change the way we interact. Which would ultimately allow the relationship to deepen. It's not like Raj and I say, "Oh, now we're happy." But we recognize that, "Oh, here we are at this time in our lives." We identify and then constantly re-evaluate what each of us wants and needs. Maybe more space, more time, more communication, more conversation, more connection.

This summer we went on a retreat together in Arizona. We committed to taking time away from home, work, family, and the day-to-day, so we could return to the original love that brought us together. And we allowed that to be our reminder of why we're still here. It doesn't mean every day is easy. It doesn't mean there are no disagreements. It means that we forget sometimes why we got together in the first place. We let life get between us. Life wasn't between us when we first met; there was this spark—this love that was blossoming. So, this year we committed to rediscovering our original love. And also being more intentional about how we communicate, which is an ongoing daily exercise.

We immersed ourselves in this beautiful resort for five days, where we listened to Gregg Braden and Bruce Lipton talk about time and spirituality and consciousness and evolution and relationships and love. We went on nature hikes and ate good food. We came back replenished. Pulling away from everything and giving yourselves time to be together is probably one of the most valuable things any couple can do on a regular basis.

That, and give each other space. Space was not something we understood early on in our marriage. Raj and I loved each other and wanted to be together all the time. We thought the more time you spent together meant you loved each other more—which makes for a good marriage, but an isolated one. I stopped hanging out with my girlfriends and traveling alone. He quit most of the hobbies he used to do alone. But this year we've recognized that each of us comes to the relationship stronger when we've had time and space away from each other. For him to do whatever he loves, and for me to do what I love. Even if it's just half a day, or a couple hours. Like, "Hey, I'm gonna go for a walk, or meditate. See ya later!" I wish every young couple would spend dedicated time together, and take space away from each other. Both are equally important!

Bruce Lipton, a scientist and consciousness leader who used to teach at Stanford University's School of Medicine, gives this analogy: the periodic table of the elements, he says, is one huge metaphor for relationships. Every element on the chart is either missing an electron or has extra electrons, so they're all spinning off-balance looking for a complementary element with which they can come together to become more balanced. Then he points out the noble gases, which are balanced on their own because they do not have extra or missing electrons. When two noble gases come together, their energy gets amplified. They don't require each other, but they amplify each other. "So," he says, "every relationship should be like a noble gas, balanced on its own first."

It's the difference between needing your partner to complete you, and entering into partnership with them as a whole and complete person. That's when you amplify each other. Once Raj and I realized this, we made the decision to shift out of neediness and into balance on our own. It takes strength, and energy—but whatever energy you put in is returned to you, amplified many times over.

My husband really stepped up to the plate this year. He's had the same career for 30 years, and for all that time he supported us financially and emotionally, a true pillar of strength. Now I have this coaching business, which is comparatively new, and as it takes off I'm getting to hold that space for him, because he's done it so beautifully for so long. It's my turn now to support him while he explores all the amazing things in this world that bring him joy aside from his career. That's the natural rhythm of life. Each of us has our own waxing and waning, and if the other person is whole and complete, they can stand that ground for us, hold that space, while we find our balance again. An absolute requirement in a healthy marriage is a balance of giving and taking.

This year we will be celebrating our 25th wedding anniversary. We're planning to travel somewhere beautiful, probably in Europe. The south of France, Portugal, Spain ... for a two or three-week vacation together. Really catch the countryside. It will be a celebration of so many major accomplishments. Our son will graduate from college next year. He is an amazing young man. Our daughter graduated high school this year and started college. She's bright and beautiful, but that's not the accomplishment. The accomplishment is that she didn't want to go far from home. She wanted to stay where she could see us, and have us be a regular part of her life. "Mommy and Daddy," she says with such sweetness, "all my friends love you. They all wish they had parents like you." And Raj and I laugh ... but when we really let it sink in, we think about how many mistakes we made, fumbling through parenthood without a manual the best we knew how. So long as we own our mistakes though, and grow from them—then we're good parents. Even with all the mistakes we've made.

So now we share the lessons we've learned with them, and remind them how perfect they are. When she gets a 100 on a test, we're like, "Wow, great, we love you." If she gets a C and dejectedly says, "I don't understand how this could have happened," we say, "You did your best and we still love you. Nothing's changed." We're teaching them they're not defined by their grades, they're not defined by their mistakes. So that's the accomplishment: when you can turn around and see two grown adults who are happy, healthy, and honoring you. It's amazing, to reflect on all the greatness in life rather than the challenges. Life is so yummy, you know?

"

Conscious Relationship is spiritual alchemy. Taking our pain and suffering of the past, our *not enoughness*, our lack of belonging, our separateness ... and together, through the mirror of another, rewriting it into gold: acceptance and celebration of the radiant and flawed wholeness of humanity.

—Megan Rose (34)
Co-founder, The Alchemy of We

We often think about relationship from an individual perspective—*What do "I" want out of relationship?* versus *What do "we" want out of relationship?* In a truly happy relationship, both partners will move from a perspective of ME to WE.

—Brave Legend (33)
Co-founder, The Alchemy of We

LINDSAY & SAMUEL & HANNAH

[Lindsay (38)—the storyteller in this chapter—is 'unofficially married' to Samuel (38). They have one kid, Oliver (8). Hannah (34) is also married to Samuel. The three adults live in a South Austin house and raise Oliver together. Lindsay's preferred word for this relationship arrangement is 'triad.']

2017

We call it a triad. Samuel is my partner and he's legally married to Hannah. He and I therefore aren't legally married, but he and I have a child together. We all live together and share everything, so in that sense, what Samuel and I have is very much a marriage. Joint checking account, co-raising a kid—all of that.

Samuel and Hannah met online in the days when online dating wasn't yet popular. They're both from Nebraska, and first hooked up when Hannah was home from school one summer. Samuel decided to follow Hannah back to school and enroll in a master's program at her college. He was accepted into the same master's program as me—he and I met in class. I knew that Samuel was dating Hannah, and I was dating someone else exclusively at the time, so we became friends only.

The next semester, Hannah studied abroad. Samuel and I started spending more time together, studying and talking late into the night. He had incredibly interesting, progressive views on all kinds of cultural norms, including marriage and monogamy. I loved to listen to him philosophize, though I was uncomfortable sometimes with how much he pushed me. He liked to get a rise out of people, and make them justify why they felt the way they did. His questions often felt more confrontational than fruitful; my impression was that he was a bit of an asshole. But then I need somebody who's an asshole in my life, or I'll roll over him.

We were always very open and vulnerable with each other, but we never crossed any lines. When I graduated before Samuel, we went our separate ways. I didn't see him again for five years.

We reconnected on Facebook. I was living in Austin by then and he was in L.A. Samuel had ended up marrying Hannah; they had what most would call an open marriage. He'd met someone else and had tried to bring her into the relationship. The three of them made a go of it, but it didn't work out. That was just ending as I came back into the picture. Prior to meeting Samuel, I didn't even know that polyamory was a thing. Initially I had zero interest in the whole business. It was not something I'd ever planned for myself.

Then Samuel shuttered his business in L.A. and he and Hannah moved to Austin. My feelings for Samuel were reignited in all of their intensity, and within two months I was pregnant. Although he and I had discussed having kids *someday*, an immediate pregnancy was never part of the plan. But it's what happened—so I had to try. Try to make it work with Samuel. Try to make it work with Hannah.

I fell into the relationship backward, and had no idea what I was getting into. I wouldn't look for it again. People ask me, "If your relationship were to end, would you want a triad again?" No, I wouldn't seek it out. I didn't intend it in the first place. It's super difficult but entirely worth it at the same time; Samuel makes it worth it. Once you're in it, it's different, I guess.

In the beginning, jealousy made everything harder. Hannah and the woman before me had competed against each other for Samuel's attention and affection. It had been ugly, and that dynamic carried over and colored our triad. It sucked, because I'd played no part in establishing that dynamic; it was old relationship baggage. Plus, the three of us happened on the heels of the three of them. Hannah hadn't had enough time to heal. That woman had moved out on April 1, and on May 1 Hannah and Samuel had moved to Austin. The aftershocks were complex.

Samuel attempted to smooth the transition by saying: "I don't want anybody here who doesn't want to be. We're just trying to make this work and I love everyone. I'm not going to make one person go away because I love someone else." It was really a call to be big people and think through our feelings. "I know we can do this," he said. "There's no need for one person to be hurt and go away because another person has joined the group." Which is much, much easier said than done.

All I knew was that I wanted to have the baby, and I wanted to have it with Samuel. I was excited to be a mom. I didn't understand how triads worked—what to do, or what not to do. How to deal with Hannah's lingering conflict—or how to tell her I would be adding a whole new layer to it. Samuel broke the news directly, the way he knew Hannah would want to hear it (which was entirely different from the way I would have wanted to find out). "How do you feel about being one big happy family?" he said in the middle of dinner one evening.

Hannah didn't respond right away, but the look on her face said, *I think I know what that means*. I found her in the kitchen later and confronted her. "I realize this is not what any of us planned," I began. "You must be upset."

"I just need time," she said.

Within 24 hours, she came back and exclaimed, "This is great!" And she was 100% sincere. Hannah doesn't know how to do anything but genuine. Both her love and her hate are total and raw. I was taken aback, but also found it refreshing that she could just assimilate the news and accept her new life. Our new life.

At the time, Hannah thought she wanted to have kids. According to her, she'd wanted a kid with Samuel since the moment they'd met, but he didn't think she was ready. She was really young when they got married. He'd been waiting until it felt like they both were ready—then I happened. Right away, Hannah said, "Well, I want to have one, too, because I've wanted to have one this whole time." After Oliver was born, however, she changed her tune. She realized she didn't want kids after all ... though she was glad to have Oliver.

In examining that myth—the story she'd been telling herself—the rest of the fable fell away. We'd assumed that, between Hannah and me, there would be two or three kids. Maybe we'd take turns, for financial reasons. But there haven't been any more kids since Oliver, who's seven now. It actually came up again this spring, while we were talking through our relationship goals and options. It would pretty much be our last chance to conceive. We collectively decided not to.

Each of us plays a different role in the home. I call myself the default parent. It's my nature to organize and control and make sure everything gets done that needs to get done. I didn't realize that was such a part of myself until I had Oliver; my tiger mom came out. Samuel is very intentional. He's always thinking ahead, planning for every situation. He's really good at "We'll want to prepare Oliver for these situations. We'll want to teach him these things down the road," while I'm managing the present. Hannah is more like Oliver's big sister. There's some conflict there, almost sibling-like in its nature. She'll babysit him if we need her to, but for the most part, she just does her own thing.

I don't think Hannah's and my relationship will ever be like what we'd envisioned: sister-wives or whatnot. Our different personalities cause us to butt heads all the time. Which is unfortunate, because in another world ... but it's the difference between potential and reality. You can't feel disappointed by what never could have been. At any rate, our relationship is much less contentious than it used to be. We used to jockey for time with Samuel or feel bitter when he chose one of us over another for the evening, but we've gotten past that. She's realized that she doesn't want to spend as much time with us; she wants more time alone, and now she gets that. And Samuel and I get time to ourselves and she gets to stay home. She stays there when Oliver goes to bed and Samuel and I can go out and do what we want to do. It's a more natural "we all get what we want" situation.

The three of us don't intentionally hide our relationship. It's not a secret—it just rarely comes up. It might be different if Hannah and I were really involved, but even then people assume that she's my sister, that she's Oliver's aunt. That's how she's known at school. People don't think twice—they don't even fathom that we might be a triad. Early on, especially when I was pregnant, my brain went to a lot of crazy places. I thought I would have to move into a separate house—that no one could know, because it might put Oliver in danger. I expected the villagers to come with their torches, but it seems like nobody cares. Nobody wants to know the details of your life; they've got their own things going on.

I was never a fan of marriage (in terms of the legal institution) to begin with, so titles don't mean much to me. I'll call Samuel my husband if the situation demands it, but I don't think of us as husband and wife otherwise. I like the word 'partner' better, but in certain circumstances that's inappropriate. Truth be told, I care so little about that stuff that it's like they can believe whatever they want. If they wouldn't guess, if it wouldn't be part of their repertoire, just let them spin on whatever.

For a while, Samuel was accused of brainwashing us, like a cult leader. The mom of the other woman before me was really upset when she found out what her daughter had gotten mixed up in. It didn't come out until the relationship dissolved, and then she made out like her daughter was a 'victim,' which was really offensive. Samuel tried to explain that everyone was there because they wanted to be. The other woman knew she should have told her family, but she didn't because it was too uncomfortable. She always said that Samuel and Hannah were her 'friends' or 'roommates' and hid behind the same kind of white lies that we use now with Oliver's teachers.

I couldn't do that with my family. We're just too close for that. Their response was surprisingly forward-thinking. "Whatever makes you happy," my mom said. "If that's working for you, then great." She's very pragmatic and worries about me financially. She did say the situation sounded like "financial suicide." Once she found out I was pregnant with Oliver, she wanted me to get an attorney to protect his rights. My dad couldn't say anything because he'd been unfaithful to my mom during their marriage. "You know that it's possible to have feelings for more than one person," I pointed out, "so who are you to judge?"

"Yeah," he agreed. "I understand that. I get it."

Not all of my friends were so understanding. A lot of them had a problem with it. The ones who weren't worth being friends with anyway fell off pretty quickly. But then you figure out who your real friends are: the ones who think and feel similarly to you; so I don't regret any of that. I've also become more secure in my relationship with time, so I don't feel the same need to discuss it with others. Some friends don't know anything about my relationship with Samuel. I don't bitch about him. There's no reason to bring him up. Again, it's not secretive, it's just not pertinent. It doesn't matter. I don't ask them about their relationship structure, either. And in some ways, we're admittedly insular. We're homebodies. We don't have parties at the house or anything.

Samuel, Hannah, and I have occasionally tried involving more people in the relationship—like, we've each gone on dating sites to see if that's something we want. I guess none of us have found it that rewarding, or an experience worth pursuing. Why would we, when we have what we want at home? It's interesting to go out and talk to other people, but I spend most of the date answering questions about how our triad works and how the new person would fit in. It's more logistical than "Let's just hang out and have fun together."

We tell Oliver everything. He knows that Hannah—whom he also thinks of as his aunt—is married to his dad, and that I'm not (and don't want to be). If he has a question, he asks and we answer him honestly. He's never asked, "Why don't my friends' dads live with two women?" or "Why is our family different?" Nothing like that. He seems to get it and is totally fine with it. My mom lives here in town and is very involved in his life. Oliver knows that she doesn't think our relationship is weird, so he just goes with it, too. I keep wondering, as he gets older and he wants to talk to other people about it, how it will go. But so far it seems okay. He's such a self-assured kid to begin with. He's been wearing rainbow fingernail polish lately and it looks awesome. The polish keeps him from picking at his nails, but when kids at school tell him, "You're a boy; why are you wearing fingernail polish?" he just says, "'Cause I want to." He's not afraid of anything. I don't know where he gets that fearlessness from, but I'm in awe of my son every day.

Some of it probably comes from his dad. Samuel is very tall, with dark hair and a beard. People perceive him as dominant, but that feels wrong knowing him as I do. One time years ago, he was wearing a black hoodie in a restaurant and this little girl at the next table over said, "That guy looks like a bad guy from a movie." Samuel was proud of that accolade. But in reality, he's incredibly sensitive. He actually doesn't think of himself as male or female. He's a very sexual person, but he's not gendered. He only uses the male pronoun because he recognizes that other people see him that way. Otherwise his outlook is pretty feminine. And feminist. Like he doesn't understand competitiveness, or sports references—he just doesn't think that way.

Samuel's felt like an outsider for his whole life. That's what prompted him to look more closely at social conventions and question why his life should have to look like everyone else's.

He's also incredibly intelligent. His memory is crazy. Almost photographic. If a subject comes up that he knows something about (which is pretty much every topic), he can expound upon it at length, enlightening people on all the details. They sometimes think he's a know-it-all, or that he's pulling it out of thin air—no one believes he could know that much about so much. But if you were to go and check his sources, you'd see he was quoting them almost verbatim.

When it's just Samuel and I, we like to go out to coffee a lot. We still talk a ridiculous amount about all kinds of things: current events, whatever's on our minds. Or we read. He's a dreamer. He's pretty ambitious, but he's also had a lot of setbacks, so he's always analyzing himself and the changes he needs to make to overcome what's holding him back. This past year he's been working through how, as a child, he didn't get what he needed from his parents. Now he's reparenting himself, telling the younger self inside him: "You're okay. You didn't get what you needed then, but now you are." It was a pretty transformative experience for Samuel, and an inspiring one to watch.

Samuel's the whole reason I entered into this 'marriage.' He had this vision for our future family that was intoxicating. I stayed because we are endlessly curious and analytical about all things—not least of which is social convention. As I've gotten older, it's been interesting observing why people do the things they do, and how often fear and social expectation take the lead. I feel confident in my situation knowing that we've all done our due diligence and understand our desires and motivations. It negates the need for rules or secrets. As my hero Mr. Rogers said, "If it's mentionable, it's manageable." We've worked hard to foster an environment where no topic is off-limits.

Because Samuel and Hannah were already married when I came into the picture, he and I felt no need to have a formal ceremony of any kind. We expressed our commitment to each other over Skype, and that was enough for me. As a young girl, I would flip through bridal magazines and pick out dresses, but that's where it stopped—at the cool 'stuff.' I never wanted to actually go through with the wedding. Not only do I hate being the center of attention, but marriage has never made sense to me conceptually. And I felt that way before my parents' divorce—it wasn't reactionary. I just remember thinking, once I understood the legal implications of marriage, *Why would anyone do that?* I wanted the fancy dress and the party; I didn't and don't want the marriage. But I do want the stability and partnership that marriage represents, and I have that now.

Sometimes people ask me if I'm jealous of Hannah because she's married to Samuel. That question doesn't compute. She signed the paperwork and wears the diamond ring, but in many ways I am closer to Samuel than she is. At the risk of comparing us again, I'll just say that I have the relationship that I want. Full stop.

About three years ago, we all started wearing wedding rings. Samuel had never worn his, and Hannah didn't feel right wearing one when her husband wasn't, but they work in different departments at the same organization and coworkers who knew they were married were always asking them why they didn't wear wedding rings. It was funny—almost like the other employees felt somehow threatened by what they didn't understand. So Samuel got a band just for appearances, and Hannah started wearing hers again. Samuel felt bad that I didn't have one, so he went out and got me a moldavite ring. It's green like an emerald, but prettier and the mythology is cooler. I feel like a hypocrite wearing it since we're not really married, but I understand that they want me to be 'part of the group.' I compromise by wearing it on my right ring finger instead of my left.

I suppose the rings serve exactly the purpose they're supposed to: they symbolize (externally) the very real and internal commitment we feel to each other. No one's going anywhere: we're here to make it work. Really, it feels like the hard work is done—all that dealing with old baggage and figuring out what we wanted our triad to look like. Now it's just the daily 'getting along' thing, and looking ahead to what's next. This marriage hasn't been the financial suicide that my mom feared, though having a kid does make everything more expensive. You'd think that three incomes would help in that department, but it doesn't. Life is expensive.

Nine years into it, I can say that my life looks vastly different from anything I'd ever imagined. But it fits me perfectly. Life with Samuel, Hannah, and Oliver is never boring (and I get bored really easily!) There's always something going on. Some new thing to think about. We've met other people in the polyamory community, and none of them have anything remotely like us. They're more into the 'open' aspect of their marriages, in that they're always seeking something 'new' or 'more' outside the relationship, as opposed to bringing someone into the existing relationship. They use titles like 'primary' and 'secondary' partners; we don't do that. We're just all together. Whereas for other polys it might be about sex, or novelty, or even romance, for us it's a life spent living together. We don't mark the years with anniversary dinners or flowers, but once a year we say, "Holy shit—it's been that long. We've come a long way!"

2018

2018 has been a busy year—and we're only a few months in. The madness is good, though. I feel better, more positive, than I did six months ago. Most of that is thanks to moving.

Until last year, we lived in what felt like the last affordable place left in Austin: a 1,200 sq. ft. house much too small for the four of us. When the rent increased dramatically it no longer made sense to live like sardines, so we started looking around. It just so happened that my mom was looking for a new place at the same time. We knew that if we all moved in together, we'd be in a better place financially ... but could we handle it emotionally?

Samuel, Hannah, my mom, and I had many conversations about every possible scenario. We expressed every fear and concern, and actually mended some old wounds in the process. After deciding it was in fact the best choice for all involved, we found a larger house in a nicer neighborhood and staked our claim. It was our first move in eight years, and felt in every way like a fresh start!

Looking back, it's easy to see how much the lack of space affected my family's relationship. Little irritations grew into resentments because there was no escape and no real privacy. With more room to spread out in, all of the adults have been able to carve out time and activities for themselves, which has helped the relationship immensely. There's no bitterness, jealousy, or left-out feelings to speak of, and our communication skills continue to improve. Of course, adding another person into the mix required extra patience during the adjustment period, but we're optimistic for the future. Financially we still have challenges, but that, too, is better than it's ever been.

Oliver just celebrated his eighth birthday. He's a little man all of a sudden, more independent every day. It's a joy to be his mother.

Most pertinent to this book: Samuel and I are still best friends and partners. We inspire and push each other to be the best versions of ourselves every day.

"

Turn to the person you love and give them a kiss and a hug, for me, right now. Just do it. One day that person will be gone and you'll wish you could touch them again.

—Jane (78)
Retired

ADAM & JENNA

[Jenna's (28) boss introduced her to his best friend, Adam (35), and the rest was history for these two formerly serial daters. Their story begins in Cincinnati, Ohio, and migrates to Chicago, Illinois.]

2016

Jenna used to have a different date almost every night of the week. She was young, attractive, and single, and had a genuinely charming personality that won over everyone she met. Corporate executives asked Jenna out, as did the Starbucks barista who made her morning mocha. Jenna said yes to them all and didn't discriminate, because at once a cynic and a romantic, she believed you could find love anywhere, but that "none of those men were probably going to work out anyway." While she waited for Mr. Right, what was the harm in enjoying a free dinner and some flattering attention?

She worked in a downtown Cincinnati skyscraper. Her boss, a kind family man, knew that Jenna was looking for love. Dare he set her up with his best and oldest friend, Adam? Adam was seven years older and outrageously funny, with a baseball obsession and a deeply rooted loyal streak. Mr. Boss decided to introduce his friend and his employee, but gave them each the independent caveat: "Caution with this one. S/he is a live wire!"

Adam and Jenna met at a Cincy art museum. There they strolled through the collections, pointing out their favorites and making fun of more abstract paintings. Before they left, they stopped in the gift shop, where Adam bought a Christmas ornament. "For our tree someday," he said. Jenna didn't know him well enough yet to differentiate between his sarcasm and sincerity, but for once, Adam was being sincere.

"I love yous were exchanged within two weeks of meeting each other," Jenna recalls. "I was obviously drawn to him early on. Then we moved in together after six months. Even though he annoys the hell out of me most days, I just knew I wanted to be with him."

Moving in together upset Jenna's conservative Catholic parents. She was 23 (going on 24); they worried she'd get pregnant. While they liked Adam, tensions remained high until he proposed a year and a half later. "I wanted her to be at least 25," explains Adam. "Old enough to know her own mind and make her own decisions." He proposed on a Hilton Head beach with the breathtaking words, "Will you make me bacon and cocktails for the rest of my life?"

Today is their one-year wedding anniversary. Here, they reflect on the First Year: expectations that were met or not met; things that were better or worse than they'd imagined.

Jenna: I thought nothing was going to change after our wedding because we'd been living together for 18 months.
Adam: But everything changed. We moved. We got a dog, so now we're parents.
Jenna: Yeah, but that was an anticipated change. I'd been campaigning for that for the year and a half we lived together.

Adam: The dog? Or moving?
Jenna: Both. It was harder than I thought. We fought a lot because of big changes like the move. I was offered a position in Chicago, so there were about two months of fighting just about the decision to move and about four months of fighting after moving.
Adam: I would say the first month after the move to Chicago there was no fighting because everything was new.
Jenna: Well two weeks of that first month we weren't living together because I moved out here without you.
Adam: I meant my first month. And then it became hard.
Jenna: But you're being a better sport about it now.
Adam: That's true.

Why did you want to get married?

Adam: Growing up, I had parents who were together and not divorced. It was how life went and what you were expected to do. This is how life goes: you get a job, you get married, you have kids.
Jenna: I used to think I'd be married at 21. Mom was like, "That's too young, you can't get married until you're 28." Then I turned 25 and we got engaged.

Can you remember having qualities or traits that you wanted in a spouse?

Adam: Yes. I definitely think that there were certain expectations I had about marriage: like a wife who can cook for kids and things like that, 'cause that's something that I always had. I found it strange when other kids got home from school and their mom wasn't there to make dinner and eat family dinners, so that was kind of important to me.

Jenna: I don't know if I thought about traits other than being good with kids. By no means was I looking to marry my father, it just sort of happened.

At what point did you start to think, 'Oh, I could marry this person,' or 'He'd be a good husband,' or 'She'd be a good wife?'

Adam: Pretty early on. In the first few weeks I was like, If this works out, I could spend my whole life with this person. I remember thinking we could get along and still have fun for a very long time. I have a unique personality, as we all do, and Jenna was able to absorb that.

Jenna: I've become a much more patient person since meeting Adam. It astounds me sometimes.

What was it like when you first moved in together?

Jenna: We fought more in those first four or five months ...

Adam: I'm sensing a pattern here: in the first four or five months after big life changes, we do not adapt well to each other. We are very selfish when big life changes happen.

Jenna: When we were dating and lived apart, we were spending almost every night together anyway, sleeping at my place or his place. Then suddenly you have this shared space and it's not your space—it's our space.

Adam: The hardest part was the bathroom. I think we fought more about the bathroom than anything else.

Jenna: I think you fought most about the bathroom with yourself.
Adam: Yeah, the bathroom is my sacred area. Don't interrupt my bathroom time. While I was getting ready, she would come in, and I don't talk until at least 9:00 a.m.
Jenna: Well because I also had to get ready for work.
Adam: But I'd be in the shower and the curtain opens, "Hi! What do you wanna do for dinner tonight?" And I don't even know what I'm wearing today, so that bothered me for quite a while. But she's gotten much better about that.
Jenna: Now we have separate bathrooms.
Adam: Separate bathrooms are very important in our relationship.
Jenna: When we have guests, I pack a bag to move into our bedroom and bathroom for a weekend, because all my clothes are in a different bedroom, too. Then he evicts me as soon as the guests leave.
Adam: I like a lot of personal space. That's a daily thing, not just inside the house. I need to be independent.
Jenna: He comes home and I just want a hug, and he's like, "Not yet."

Did you guys have conversations about life goals or kids before getting married?

Adam: We both knew we wanted children, so that wasn't a big issue. I think we talked about it in the beginning, like, "What do you want to do?" That was mostly a question from me to Jenna, because I knew Jenna was pretty career-oriented. Now, more than ever, she's committed to staying at this company—

because she's doing well, and they compensate very well, which is nice for us to take kids places and do fun things with them.

Jenna: The only disagreement is the time we have kids. He would have liked to have had kids four years ago.

Adam: Well, I'm old. And she was 23 when I met her.

Jenna: You were just a few weeks from turning thirty.

Adam: And that freaked me out. I didn't know she was 23 going into our blind date. But I was more concerned because me at 23 was very different from Jenna at 23.

Jenna: Yeah, because I exude maturity.

Adam: Sometimes, unless you're around your parents.

Were you concerned about him being older?

Jenna: No, I assumed he was around thirty when we met because my boss was around 30. That didn't bother me.

Adam: I had dated plenty of 23-year-old women, so I assumed that what she wanted then would be different in two years, and being 29, I was like, *Do I waste my time? She's probably gonna change.*

Have you seen Jenna change?

Adam: Yeah. She's become much more confident, in a professional sense. She's much less concerned about what other people think about her. She pushes back a lot more now, too, but she still has her pouty temper tantrums and there's nothing I can do other than be like, "I wanna leave the house," and that pisses her off even more. When she has her pouty temper tantrums she won't speak. She just sits with a scowl on her face.

Jenna, have you seen Adam change in the last four years?

Jenna: Yeah. So Adam's been complaining about his job since I met him, regardless of what kind of job it was. When I first met him, he worked at T-Mobile, and he continued to just be miserable and do the same job for the next three years. But now that he's gotten a new job in Chicago, I think he sees that he has options.
Adam: Yeah, I think now that I've made one change, it's easier to make other ones.
Jenna: You've realized you don't have to be miserable for the rest of your life.

How do you guys show each other that you love each other?

Jenna: I make you dinners, I clean the house for you, and then you tell me that you don't really care about those things. Acts of service are my way of expressing love.

When do you feel most loved by your husband?

Jenna: I don't know.
Adam: Hugs. Unsolicited.
Jenna: Yeah, because normally I have to ask for them. How do you feel most loved by me?
Adam: I feel most loved by you when you surprise me. Like you left work early today and picked up a roast,

and said, "We're having steak-and-ale pie tonight," and I was like, "Oh, that's impressive."

Jenna: I told you four days ago that we were gonna do that for dinner. He doesn't really listen when I tell him things.

Adam: Yeah, but I don't know, it still felt good. I don't think Jenna has to express that as much because I don't look for that, I don't need affirmation.

Jenna: I would like some more affirmation in my life.

Adam: I know you would.

Jenna: Only once in the history of our relationship has he surprised me with flowers and that was two weeks into knowing me.

Adam: That's not true. I've brought them home in Cincinnati.

Jenna: Okay, twice.

Adam: I'm just not really a flowers guy and you understood my point of view when I said, "Flowers are kind of dumb because they die right away."

Jenna: It's just the act of being surprised with something small and beautiful.

Adam: "Surprise! It's dead." I just think there are other surprises that could be better for you.

Jenna: Like what?

Adam: Like you need new sunglasses. Something useful. I struggle to purchase things that just go away.

Adam, you said when you were thinking of marriage as you were growing up, you had the idea of the nuclear family: two parents raising kids. So what do you think about kids? Why do you want them? What does that mean to you?

Adam: I just like being around kids. They're really

entertaining. I grew up with a lot of kids around the house because my mother was always a stay-at-home mom, so we were the house in the neighborhood with the doors always open. The kids from down the street would come into our house and just rifle through the pantry because they knew my mom would have stocked up the cupboard. I'm just used to being around children and I love their imagination.

Jenna: When we have people over at our house who have kids, I'll end up talking to the adults after dinner and he'll be chasing the children around the living room for the rest of the night.

Adam: I find that more entertaining than most of the adults.

Jenna: I think babies are cute and snuggly and as soon as they start talking, Adam can take over.

Adam: That's when I want to be in charge.

Jenna: He thinks they're boring until they can talk. That's when I'm like, "Oh, man, I actually have to entertain you."

Adam: So once they start talking, I can stop working and come home and take them to school. I would be great at parent-teacher conferences.

Jenna: No, you wouldn't listen to what the teacher was saying.

Adam: "Adam, today Cardinal said, 'What the fuck? Why do we have to do this?' Can you tell us about that?" That's our kid's name. Cardinal.

Jenna: No. No. No.

Adam: Red?

Jenna: No.

So sports are something you guys share.

Adam: Well, we kind of share it.
Jenna: I learned to be a good sport about them. I don't want to watch sports every day.
Adam: She'll attend. She won't be invested, but she'll attend.
Jenna: To spend time with you. He's social with other people.
Adam: I do appreciate that, too.
Jenna: I would like more shared interests. Sometimes I have to push you to do things, like riding bikes.
Adam: I like riding bikes, but I've always considered that an alone-time kind of thing, like a decompression kind of thing.
Jenna: On the contrary, every time I rode bikes when I was growing up it was a family thing.
Adam: It makes me nervous riding bikes with Jenna because she's a road hazard, whether it be on foot, pedal, or vehicle. It just makes me nervous. She will get hurt, and in turn, so will lots of other people.
Jenna: Shouldn't that make you more inclined to ride with me? What if I wipe out on my own?
Adam: I just think you shouldn't ride bikes until we live in a safe community with a bike route.

How have you guys divided tasks, like domestic chores or taxes?

Adam: I did the taxes but Jenna stood over my shoulder the entire time not trusting me to do it.
Jenna: Well that's because I deal with our finances, and I just wanted to know what was going on—I'd never done taxes before. This year, I think we should go to an accountant. This was a complicated year. Moving, landlord; I feel like an accountant could get us the

best return.
Adam: I feel like I can do that.
Jenna: In general I handle most of the finances and bills.
Adam: It's just like a fatherly thing. We're supposed to do the taxes.
Jenna: I also do the cooking and cleaning. He's supposed to do dishes and garbage.
Adam: I would do a lot more cooking if we had grill access. I don't necessarily like cooking.
Jenna: But that's why you bought a George Foreman.
Adam: But that's not grilling and that thing sucks. The neighbors downstairs have an actual tailgate grill, with a little flame propane thing. I think that we should get one of those for Hanukah.
Jenna: Who's gonna take out the garbage?
Adam: I take out the garbage. However, you need to inform me when I need to take out the garbage instead of me waking me up and running late to work and there are two bags of garbage siting in the living room.

What is your fighting style, and how do you work it out?

Adam: I'm more of a fists kinda guy, she likes to use the feet. (Pause.) All of our fights are just verbal disagreements.
Jenna: He gets mean, and says mean things, and then I get pouty and sulky.
Adam: Well, that's not always how it works. Maybe that's how you perceive it in your head. I feel like most of our fights start when she gets pouty. I don't stop pestering her until she'll speak.

Jenna: You say some mean things.
Adam: Why don't you talk to me? You need to be an adult.
Jenna: You don't poke me with a smile on your face. You say things in a very sassy way.

Jenna, what are three strengths you think you bring to the relationship?

Adam: Cooking, cleaning, and pouting.
Jenna: Responsibility, like follow-through. When I say we're going to do something, we're going to do it.
Adam: I have to argue.
Jenna: I only listed one strength and you're already arguing? What's your counter-argument to that?
Adam: It's the follow-through that I don't always agree with.
Jenna: What do you mean?
Adam: I feel like there are many tasks that I have asked you to do or we know are coming up and you procrastinate until they're almost too late. Like you wouldn't return your wetsuit. You almost cost us $200 because you refused to return the wetsuit, and then I did it myself and we had one day left to do it when I checked in.
Jenna: That's one instance.
Adam: How long have your expensive sunglasses been broken, for which you were eligible to get a 50% discount on a replacement pair?
Jenna: They still work fine.
Adam: And now that window has what?
Jenna: Closed.
Adam: And how long have I been bringing that up to you?

Jenna: Four months.
Adam: At least. So let's temper the follow-through.
Jenna: Okay, responsibility though.
Adam: Isn't that a responsibility?

Okay, Adam, so one of your strengths is being a realist. Jenna, what are two more strengths you contribute?

Jenna: Optimism/positivity to balance out his pessimism.
Adam: Realism. Yeah that can be a clash sometimes such as, "Hey, let's take the dog to the farmer's market." My response is, "Yeah ... farmer's markets are crowded, the dog is kinda crazy still, those two things combined could cause the farmer's market to be a stressful place."
Jenna: You did not phrase that so eloquently! You were like, "No, that's a stupid idea. Why would we do that? Discussion over."
Adam: Then I told you the dog is crazy and it is crowded.
Jenna: But you say it with this sassy attitude, and that's how fights begin.
Adam: Well, you'll just have to accept it. So we went, 'cause Jenna always wins.
Jenna: Who was pouting the entire time?
Adam: You. You were extremely irritated at the dog and the crowd.
Jenna: Also at your attitude.
Adam: Yeah. But I was right. But you did go into it extremely optimistic, I will give you that.
Jenna: I feel like I challenge you. I challenge you to do things that most of the time you end up thanking

me for.
Adam: Yeah. That happens often.
Jenna: Getting you out of your comfort zone, moving to Chicago, getting you to ride bikes ...
Adam: I have to be honest; I still have not thanked you for moving me to Chicago. And I'm not sure that I will.
Jenna: No, there have been some moments where you say, "You know, I really like this city. Outside of work, I enjoy the city."
Adam: I do like the city. I think I would have enjoyed it much better if I was 27 also though.
Jenna: Mentally, we're around the same age.

What makes the city different at 33?

Adam: I don't know, I'm just kind of past the busy, need-to-explore-something-new-every-single-moment-of-the-day point in my life.
Jenna: Because you're a grouchy old man?
Adam: I don't think that's it.

Adam, what are some strengths or values that you bring to the relationship?

Adam: I think my humor is important to our relationship, and sometimes on lazy days I can make Jenna lie on the couch and laugh. Another strength would be I have the ability to make new friends and engage new people in the conversation, so if it's just the two of us and there's no one else around, we can go to a random restaurant, or a bar, and I can draw people into conversations and learn about new things that maybe we wouldn't have otherwise.

What are some goals or dreams you have for the next 5 years?

Jenna: Adam would like to move back to Cincinnati in a year and six months, and start having kids immediately.
Adam: What are your hopes and dreams for the next 5 years?
Jenna: I think a lot of mine are career-driven. I have no idea where my career will take me in the next 5 years. Yes, we will have the option to move back to Cincinnati, but I'd also like to move to Toronto and you keep shooting that one down.
Adam: We are not moving to Canada, it's not going to happen.
Jenna: It'd be awesome.
Adam: It wouldn't. We're not moving north.
Jenna: We are going to make a weekend trip to Toronto though.
Adam: I'd rather go to Montreal.
Jenna: We do have an office in Montreal, but I don't speak French.
Adam: You don't have to. They speak English there. What are your goals for me in the next 5 years?
Jenna: Stop being a grouchy old man.
Adam: What do you think will make me stop being a "grouchy old man?"
Jenna: Being a stay-at-home dog dad. I don't know, I want you to find something that you enjoy doing for work, whether that's staying in banking or something else. I get so much joy from my job, I want you to be able to experience something similar, especially because we spend so much of our lives at work.
Adam: I agree.

Jenna: When you have good days at work, you're enjoyable to be around at home. When you have bad days at work, you're not enjoyable to be around at home.
Adam: That's because I get home and you're like, "How was your day at work?" and then I have to rehash it. I prefer to leave work at work.
Jenna: I can't ask how your day was?
Adam: You can, but you probably shouldn't.

Was your wedding what you had envisioned? Was it the wedding you'd dreamed about?

Jenna: Yeah. I wish we'd had a videographer, because even now it's only been a year and there are so many things that I don't remember about the day. I was just so caught up in the moment, I blinked and our ceremony was over. I do not remember the words we said to each other because there was so much anxiety and emotion happening. Other than that, I thought it was a great time. Everyone said it was such a fun wedding and they had such a great time, which makes me happy. The only thing I would have changed is I wish Adam didn't have so many whiskeys.
Adam: I had a blast.
Jenna: I had to help him out of his tuxedo as he was falling asleep on the couch in our hotel room.
Adam: Yeah, that was a fun night.

How'd you pick your rings?

Adam: Jenna went with her friend downtown and they picked out a $5,000 dollar ring itself before the diamond was involved.

Jenna: We went to a very expensive jewelry shop, but it was downtown, it was convenient, we could walk down at the lunch hour, just so I could get a sense of what I wanted. The round solitaire looked best on my finger.
Adam: She came home with the card and said, "This is what I like," and I scoffed at it, threw the card on the ground.
Jenna: Okay, back up. You told me that I should go to the jewelry store to figure out what I wanted. You did not want to ring shop with me because then I would know exactly what I was getting so I should go by myself and get a sense of what I wanted and come back and tell you, so I came back and said, "I would like a solitaire with a simple diamond band, and here is one that I really like."
Adam: It upset me that she said, "This is exactly what I want." So she had picked it out herself and I threw it on the ground, she pouted and went upstairs, and I picked it up and put it in my pocket.
Jenna: I don't remember that.
Adam: Then I went to the jewelry store, showed them what I was interested in, and they said, "We have something very similar to that, almost the exact same, just not the same brand." I was not planning to purchase a ring that day but I did.

What does the ring mean to you? Do you look at it and think of each other? Do you forget you're wearing it?

Adam: No, I always know I'm wearing it. I think it's surprisingly more symbolic than I expected.
Jenna: Man, I'm stuck with him forever.
Adam: I mean, this isn't Saudi Arabia. There are laws

that allow you to get out of this state.

What are your views on fidelity?

Jenna: We don't have an open marriage, if that's what you're asking.
Adam: I don't think that there should be a view on it; I think that it is what it is—you don't stray from your partner.
Jenna: I'm not planning to go around and be with anybody else.
Adam: Would you care to expand on that?
Jenna: I'll remain true to you.
Adam: It sounds like you'll try to.
Jenna: Stop trying to overanalyze my words!

Do you plan to do anything to celebrate your one-year?

Adam: I don't think we have Monday night plans. We can go to Los Tres Panchos and have some delicious tacos. Tacos 'til I die.
Jenna: No, we don't have any other plans. It's just been a really busy fall and summer, a lot of out-of-town weekends and people coming to visit.
Adam: I'm really looking forward to having multiple weekends of no plans. Jenna's very much a planner, she likes having set schedules and things to do.
Jenna: I mean we had to have a set schedule this summer with so many things going on.
Adam: Why are you sounding so defensive? I didn't accuse you of anything; I'm just saying you like having plans.
Jenna: You made it sound like I forced you into four

months of plans.

Adam: I mean, things fell the way the fell. I like not having any plans on the weekend and I can wake up and say, "I feel like doing this," and then an hour later you're like, "I don't really want to do this anymore, let's do this."

Jenna: That doesn't have anything to do with celebrating our one-year. Because it's been so busy, we haven't been planning anything in a big way. I feel like we will celebrate our one year in February when we go to Hawaii.

Jenna had just received a travel voucher for being one of the top five salespeople in her company in 2016. She planned to use it to go to Hawaii; the couple ended up traveling to Europe instead, in March 2017.

2017

What's the last year been like for you?

Jenna: After moving to Chicago last year to fill an open position, I just got promoted again. It validated why we moved here and has set me up for possible future promotions. Adam stopped complaining about living in Chicago after that. He stopped resenting it because he could see the long game.

Adam: I switched jobs and made friends. However, when Jenna took her new job, she immediately began a strong uptick in complaining. She did not like her role and responsibility in the beginning.

Jenna: Now I hardly ever bring work home. You're welcome.

Adam & Jenna

Adam: Yeah, but you still work just as late.
Jenna: No, it takes 40 minutes to get home now.
Adam: I actually really like Chicago. I don't love the fact that I don't get the same amenities. Like space. I need a backyard. In many ways, big cities are very convenient because you can do things quickly and closely; but in some ways, Cincinnati was more convenient because I could just get in the car and get things done without having to travel 45 minutes to move a couple miles in traffic.
Jenna: It's been good for your career. You actually have a career path now.
Adam: I'm not very concerned about that.

Jenna, you just won an award at work. Tell me about that.

Jenna: We used the money to go to London and Ireland in March. London's overrated but Ireland is awesome.
Adam: Yeah, we had somewhat different expectations of the trip. You weren't happy with certain things I wanted to do.
Jenna: All you wanted to do was drink in pubs.
Adam: That's what you do in Ireland. You meet people and have a drink with them. I'm a big social, let's-talk-to-people guy.
Jenna: It was supposed to be a romantic getaway.
Adam: We should have gone somewhere romantic then.
Jenna: I wanted to go to Hawaii. You picked Europe. Regardless, it was still a trip for two and you just wanted to talk to old dudes.
Adam: I wanted the Ireland experience. You wanted

the Jenna-and-Adam experience.
Jenna: Is that unreasonable to expect?
Adam: No.
Jenna: I drug him home from pubs before he wanted to leave every night. But probably by the time that he needed to come home.

Do you have any other travel plans?

Jenna: I'm looking forward to Turks and Caicos for his cousin's wedding. But I also want to plan another trip, just the two of us.
Adam: The French Riviera or Italy.
Jenna: Napa.
Adam: I'm fine with that, too. I've never even been to the West coast.
Jenna: And Denver. Or Yosemite. You can do Napa and Yosemite in the same trip. A few days in the national park then go to wine country.
Adam: Your idea of time and tasks and the space and ability to get those done is sometimes overly ambitious.
Jenna: I have vacation days.

Two years in, what are your views on marriage?

Jenna: Longest two years of my life.
Adam: I think we're more honest and open with each other. At least Jenna is.
Jenna: I just call you out on your shit more?
Adam: No, you tell me what you want and need.
Jenna: I may or may not get it, though. Like words of affirmation. If I want them, I should get them. Same with quality time. The thing is, I would need so much

less time with you if the time you gave me was actually quality.
Adam: You want me to just sit down and give you 3,000 words all at once and then you'd be good for the week?
Jenna: For my birthday in April, all I wanted was a love letter, because he never wrote one on our wedding day. It took him until the morning of my birthday to actually write one, which he sent to me via email. It was good, but I shouldn't have had to ask 50,000 times.
Adam: People be busy, yo.
Jenna: He seemed to be genuine in it, which is an emotion I don't get from him often. But he's also continued to show his love with gifts, which is his love language. He's brought me home a lot of surprises this summer.
Adam: Shirts. Clothes she likes. Jewelry.
Jenna: I've liked everything you've given me, but if you just looked at me in the morning and sincerely said, "I love you, I hope you have a great day," you'd never have to spend any money on me ever.
Adam: But when I get you a gift, it's because I'm thinking of you and I love you.
Jenna: But it doesn't fill my love tank.
Adam: Buy a new tank.

Have you developed any new shared interests this year?

Jenna: We've been building Legos.
Adam: I've always been obsessed. I played with them as a kid all the time. I loved building model cities. Finally I just bought one and we built it and she was like, "Yeah, that was actually pretty fun."

Jenna: It was for the first two times. Now I would like to do other things.
Adam: It was therapy. You can let everything go from your week. It's rewarding.
Jenna: He did actually sit down with me for two straight hours.
Adam: We both build at the same time, each doing a page. Our marriage is democratic that way. But like, she's the executive branch, and I'm a mix between judicial and congress.
Jenna: I don't understand what the different branches of government do.
Adam: ... You know that's recorded, right?

What was the last date you went on?

Adam: We spent a weekend in Michigan recently.
Jenna: And a couple weekends ago, we had a whole date weekend. We did dinner and a movie Friday. Got pedicures Saturday. Went to a baseball game. We haven't had a date night since then.
Adam: I've been working the last few weekends. We always get together and watch *Game of Thrones* on Sunday. You made a charcuterie plate.
Jenna: You complained about the charcuterie.
Adam: The salami selection was not good. There was something wrong with it. Plus, it's not a meal.

Do you have any advice for other married couples?

Jenna: Don't expect marriage to be a honeymoon. Marriage is just harder than I ever expected. I just feel like in general we used to be happier together. I really enjoyed our date weekend—when we focused on

each other—but when we don't focus, it's not a great marriage.
Adam: I feel Jenna takes her ideal of marriage 100% from her mother and father, who do everything together. They go to the same restaurant together every Friday night. I'm more independent. I don't need to do everything, like go to the grocery store, together.
Jenna: I like grocery shopping together. Plus, if I forget something, then you're equally to blame. Your parents don't seem to do as much together. I've never seen them grocery shop together. I've never heard your parents talk about going on a date together.

What's going right in your marriage?

Jenna: Adam sometimes still makes me laugh.
Adam: I make you laugh all the time.
Jenna: You make yourself laugh all the time.
Adam: True. You gotta entertain yourself.

Do you have goals for 2018?

Adam: Jenna sent me a list of goals at the beginning of the year.
Jenna: I did. One of them was increasing our savings account, and we've exceeded my annual goal.
Adam: You also said, "Find a hobby to do together that doesn't involve TV." Which we did: Legos.
Jenna: I enjoy the concept of Legos, but not how expensive they are for how quickly you build them.
Adam: I'm a Lego savant. I'll slow down. What if we create a mini-Adam? That would be fun.
Jenna: Vacations before babies. That's the whole point of planning trips now. Napa. Or we could plan

a ski trip.
Adam: I don't like skiing. I don't like doing things I don't excel at immediately.
Jenna: But you'll excel at parenthood? Not until you agree to change 50% of the diapers.
Adam: I'll change them when I have to. It just takes getting used to. I almost threw up every time I had to pick up dog poop in the beginning.
Jenna: We'll see.

Update: In 2018, Jenna was promoted yet again and the couple relocated to Bentonville, Arkansas—a city they feel is the perfect place for starting a family. They still collect holiday ornaments. Recent additions to the collection include a Guinness ornament from Ireland, bears from Harrod's in London, and one from the Anheuser-Busch factory in St. Louis. As is apparent in this interview, Jenna and Adam also still love to verbally spar—but it's all good-natured.

“

Last night, I made out with my husband. I haven't kissed him like that in three years. That's 1,095 days. 1,095 days of not being close. Of not seeing him truly. Of not allowing myself to love him. And not allowing him to love me.

I've ALWAYS wanted a Great Love. It was inscribed on my husband's wedding ring that he never wears. The pink morganite stone of my engagement ring represents soul and divine love. I never wear it either.

Until now.

After we kissed last night, my husband turned to me and said, “You kissed me like you remember that you love me.”

—Judy (39)
Writer & business strategist

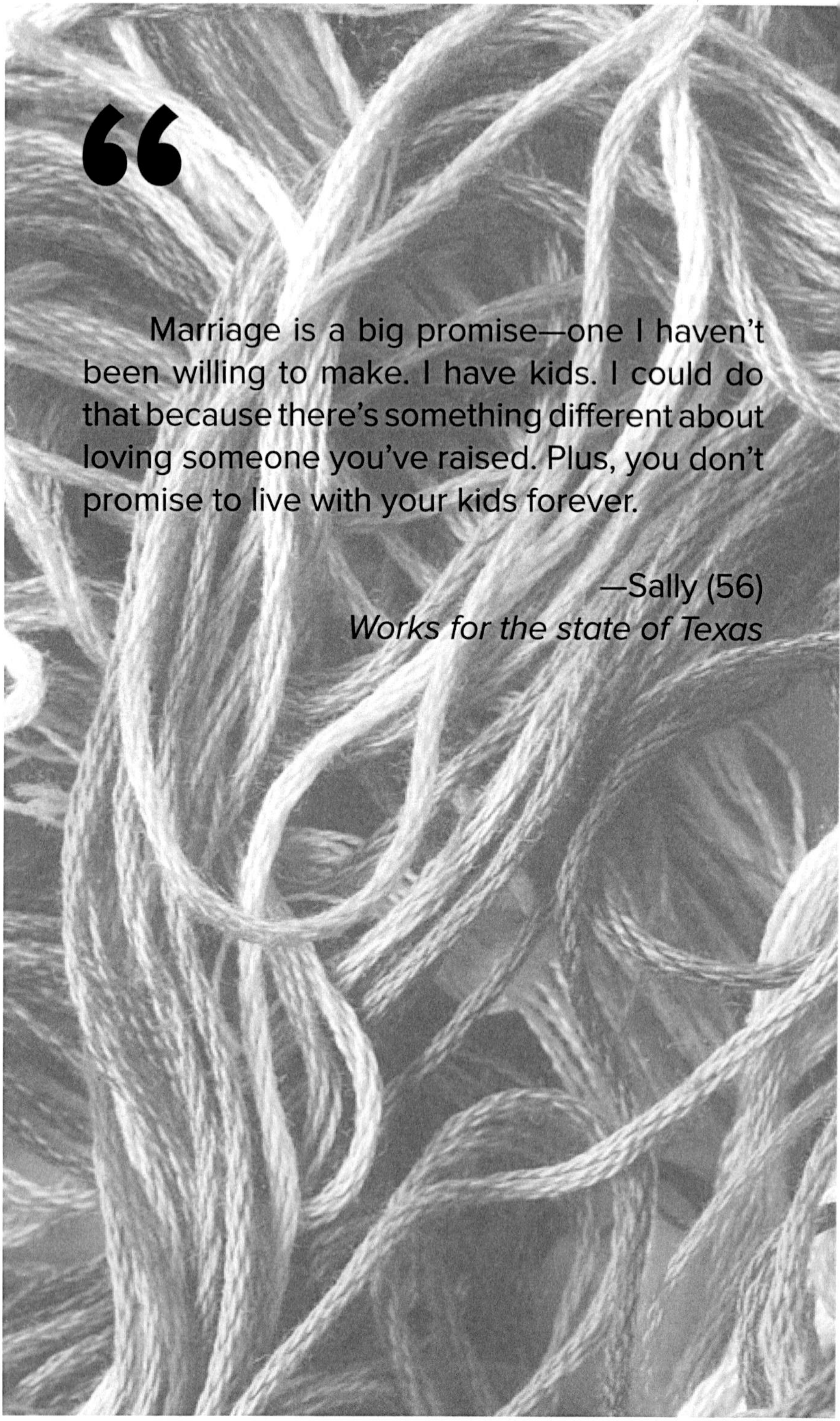

“

Marriage is a big promise—one I haven’t been willing to make. I have kids. I could do that because there’s something different about loving someone you’ve raised. Plus, you don’t promise to live with your kids forever.

—Sally (56)
Works for the state of Texas

BETH & SANDY

[Beth (69) and Sandy (74) met in a Colorado bookstore. Both teachers, they bonded over their love of learning and seeing kids succeed—often in the most unconventional fashions. Now happily retired, they have yet to stop adventuring.]

2017

Beth: It was 1975. I was working in the mountains of Georgetown, Colorado. On my afternoon off, I wandered into the local bookstore. That's where I saw Sandy, browsing the shelves with a friend of mine who introduced us. An avalanche on the pass had prevented them from going skiing that day. Now Sandy was doing research for a class that she was going to teach. I watched her pick up the book *Stampede to Timberline*, which I had also read, and being flip said, "Don't buy that book. It's in the library." Polly, the bookstore owner and one of my friends, mumbled, "Thanks a lot, Beth." Sandy didn't buy the book that day, so I gave her a copy signed by Polly for our anniversary a few years later.

Sandy: I was getting ready to teach a senior seminar in January. We were going to take the kids to Mexico to do an Outward Bound course. The program was different every semester. Some years we stayed with Native American families in Arizona; other times we backpacked the whole semester. The program I was researching in the bookstore that day was called "Colorado goes Bi" (for the bicentennial). It required the kids to do research in old mining towns and compile oral histories. Anyway, I didn't think much of that first meeting with Beth, but several weeks later I met up with another mutual friend, Ellen, for dinner. As I was lamenting that we needed more teachers for the program, Ellen said, "Why don't you call Beth? She has her master's in education and she's adventurous; she might want to do that."

Beth: I thought the program sounded interesting, but I was really sold when my alma mater in Denver, Loretto Heights College, agreed to give me education credits toward my Colorado teaching certificate. So off we went to Mexico on a bus with 45 kids and four teachers. The drive alone took two and a half days. The teachers took turns driving and sleeping and making sure that the kids had gotten rid of anything that could have gotten us in trouble at the border. Once in Mexico, the roads were bad and our map was worse. It was the middle of the night; I was driving and Sandy was riding shotgun, when all of a sudden we saw a white horse rear up on the side of the road. It was pitch dark. I thought maybe I was hallucinating. "Did you see that?" I asked her.

Sandy: "Yeah." Beth stopped the bus. There wasn't any traffic, so we pulled over slowly. In the headlights we could just see that the road had ended and we were twenty feet from a dry riverbed. (There was no horse.) Had we hit that bed going 45 miles an hour, you can bet all the kids would have woken up. Instead it was a little bit of excitement and a neat shared experience between Beth and me. Once we got to our destination, we didn't see each other at all except midway through when the kids were doing their solos; then we had three days together. Otherwise Beth took her 10 kids and I took mine and we all charted a different route across the Mexican desert, along the Sea of Cortez.

Beth: Then we drove home and did the 'Colorado Goes Bi' program next, which Sandy and I taught together. We had no days off while teaching this program. On the weekends we'd take the kids up in the mountains to go cross-country skiing. One weekend a member of the school board called to ask why a public school bus was driving over a pass on a Saturday. They thought we'd kidnapped the bus!

Sandy: That spring, we took the kids to a Navajo reservation in Arizona. We'd gotten to know each other by then and had begun to be attracted to each other and care about each other. One night we had a campfire by the bus and we were listening to "Send in the Clowns" by Judy Collins. (That's kind of our heart-strings-song. The music and the lyrics reflected the absurdity of where we were and the magic of the moment.) That was when we knew we had something. It took from the time we met in December until April to develop a relationship. Neither of us was looking for a relationship, but we just kept having good times, challenging times, philosophically educational times, and interesting conversations.

Beth: It was such a fertile time of discovery. Sandy thought I knew a lot more about mountaineering than I did. She'd assumed that because I had a great pair of boots and lived in the mountains when we met, I knew what I was doing when it came to backpacking. I'd been a camp counselor, but in Ohio—where it's flat. It was near a lake so I knew about canoeing, but I didn't know anything about backpacking and mountains. On the Outward Bound trip to Mexico, all of our patrols climbed the mountain Tepopa. Explaining the route, Sandy said, "Take the kids up toward the saddle," and I'm like, *What the hell's a saddle?* I only knew horse saddles. I learned a lot really quickly. Luckily we didn't lose any kids.

Sandy: We did a lot of backpacking and hiking together after that. We started retreating to Beth's cabin in the mountains, where we'd play guitar and plan our next module. Nature was our church; spirituality infused everything we did. Beth had grown up Catholic, but there in our little hideaway we slowed down and found intention and belief and mystery all around us. I was in my late 20s and Beth was in her mid-20s. To have that experience of working and getting paid to do what you love to do—outside all day, working with kids, rafting the Colorado River ... we were loose on the world and free, wandering wherever we wanted.

Beth: Anytime you can integrate nature with education, it's so special. Getting to teach inner-city kids in the great outdoors really cemented and enlivened our relationship. If we had just been in a classroom, I don't know if it would've worked out the same way. We both really enjoyed witnessing what Mother Nature taught those kids. They came from diverse economic groups, but one and all were scared at night of the dark. There was no electricity. They couldn't curl their hair. But they came to love nature and crave it, and it was such an empowering gift to be a part of opening kids' eyes to that.

Sandy: We ran into some kids years later who'd done that program. I don't know if any of them recognized the beginnings of our relationship at the time, but when they saw us together in a restaurant ten or fifteen years later, they immediately knew and accepted it and loved it. They told us what a life-changing experience the trips had been. We hope it was like that for all those kids.

Beth: After school let out, we drove our little green Datsun truck, loaded down with a tent and a Yamaha 175, to the Pacific Northwest. We camped along the California, Oregon, and Washington coasts with the intention of camping free all summer. I think we were on the Olympic Peninsula in Washington when we camped a little too close to the ocean. The tide came in and almost went in our tent. "Let's live together," Sandy said suddenly—a proposal for which I was entirely unprepared. I had a job lined up in Michigan for the fall. "Well, what would we do if we lived together?" I asked. It's a question that has been quoted back to me many times over the years. The answer was: "Well, we can have a ranch and have fences and raise kids, llamas, horses, alpacas and have a B&B."

Sandy: I'd been thinking about moving in together for a while, and was surprised when the question seemed to catch Beth off-guard. She felt she needed to keep her word to the program in Michigan, so she left me until January. I wrote her letters every week, trying to convince her to move back to Denver. I even went to visit her once, when we went to an education conference in Toronto. That's when she let me know she'd be coming back. In those days—1977—gay marriage wasn't a thing. It didn't even occur to me that it was a life that I could have. We had lots of gay friends who lived with their partners, but no one talked about marriage. I told my brother and sister-in-law that I was with Beth—with a woman—and when they took it in stride I came out to my mom. She had a harder time with it. Beth's parents, on the other hand ...

Beth: Yeah, my parents would have sent us a cake. But I wasn't really talking to them at the time. I was a bit of a radical and unglued. I was angry. Sandy kept asking, "How come you don't like your parents? They're great!" Sure, but my father was an alcoholic and my mother was too for a while and all I could think about was getting out. So after college, I didn't go back home, except maybe for Christmas every once in a while. I worked in the ghetto in Cleveland and campaigned for civil rights and felt this moral obligation to change the world. That my father took pride in what I did made me angry, because I didn't want him to—I didn't feel he was entitled to do that. Meeting Sandy softened me and made me a better person. She helped me to understand my parents more. Then they stopped drinking and I was able to be a better family member and they loved it. Sandy gets all the credit for that.

Sandy: Jack [Beth's dad] and I shared a special bond over history. He was quite the history buff and he gave me the A-OK right away. He and Mary [Beth's mom] bought a tree farm in Florida and the first time I visited the tree farm I was just blown away because I had one brother and Beth has six brothers and sisters, and they were all there. It was the spring after Beth came back to Denver. As overwhelming as the trip was, I felt that everyone accepted me and figured out who I was pretty quickly. I came to feel like Jack and Mary were my second mom and dad.

Beth: In fact, Mom always says that I can't come visit her again unless I bring Sandy. It gives me an idea that Sandy's the better part of me.

Sandy: So we moved in together in 1977. Things were pretty normal. We both worked. From the get-go we were building things. I don't think we've lived in a house where we didn't build a fence, or a greenhouse, or changed the roof or something. Later that year I was on a plane and read an article about the Shelter Institute in Bath, Maine, which was offering a class on how to build a passive solar timber-frame house. My dad was a builder and I loved building. I immediately thought, *We're going to do this. We're going to find some land in the mountains—enough land to build a camp for kids, and a house.* A few months later, we bought the first forty acres.

Beth: We started building in 1978—figuring everything out as we went along. We slept in a tent on the property, spent every weekend working, and went into town for a beer on Saturday nights. Our original intention was just to learn how to do it: how to build our timber frame house.

Sandy: On our way home from the Shelter Institute, we'd stopped at Walden Pond, inspired by Thoreau's quote that humans should build their own homes as birds build their own nests. We placed a stone from Walden Pond, as well as a Susan B. Anthony dollar with the quote "Failure is impossible," in the corner pier of our foundation. Hopefully it will be there for a long time.

Beth: We wanted our mountain place to be a free camp for kids, and for a while, it was. They lived in teepees on our land and we continued working in Denver during the school year. After we learned to build fences and raise cattle, then we added livestock to the ranch. In the early 1990s, we decided we wanted to run a bed and breakfast, even though we knew nothing about it. We started building on an addition in 1992. It took us 3 summers (15 months all together) to finish it and we opened for business in 1995.

Sandy: I resigned from teaching in 1996. Friends asked, "How do you know how to do all of this?" And I said, "You just start. You just learn. I can't cook very well, and my mother said, 'Can you do that?' and I said, 'I can do this, Mom.'" We stayed at B&Bs around the country to learn what was good and what was not good, and we learned more about what was not good because the people who owned them weren't there. They had people who made the beds and made breakfast and you never saw the owners and we didn't want ours to be that way. We wanted ours to be us. So we ran it for 18 years and hosted people from all over the world. According to our guest books, people loved it. We won several awards for best B&B in Colorado and it was really cool.

Beth: We talked about having kids of our own someday; in the meantime, there were too many kids at school who needed us. Intermittently, we kept kids who couldn't go home for whatever reason. They'd turn up on our doorstep having run away from an abusive situation across town. We always had kids chilling out and wishing they lived with us, but the closest we ever got was being godparents. Looking back on it, I think it was for the best. We've had all the kids we've taught and worked with, and our nieces and nephews, and lots of dogs—and I don't have to send them to college, so ...

Sandy: Part of it was that we couldn't have had kids together, right? Not being married, we couldn't even buy a house or a car together. We actually didn't think about getting married until the Defense of Marriage Act was undone.

Beth: Well, we thought about it before then politically as a cause. When DOMA did go down, I said to Sandy, "I think we should get married, because if they try and take that away again, I want to be in the way!" It was my old radical self rising up again instead of staying comfortable and ducking. So that's when we actually started thinking about getting married.

Sandy: The support from our families was amazing. Our nephew Michael got so excited the day that DOMA was declared illegal, he called his mom [Beth's sister, Sara] and said, "We have to call Beth and Sandy! DOMA just fell!" All of our nieces and nephews, no matter their political views (we've got some that consider themselves pretty conservative Republicans and some Democrats) have come to see us as two people who just love each other very much. Michael told his mom, "I want to have a relationship like Beth and Sandy."

Beth: Those moments are pretty wonderful. The Millennial generation is so much less concerned about all that, and you see kids coming up with more open and accepting perspectives than we had before.

Sandy: We got married on May 3, 2014. We always celebrated our 'anniversary' on May 1, but we honeymooned in Costa Rica the week prior to getting married, so we chose May 3 instead. I was 71 and Beth was 66. The next year—our first wedding anniversary—marked 40 years of being together. I proposed first, over Christmas in Florida. I got down on one knee, gave Beth a ring. When we announced it to Beth's mom, she said—

Beth: She was like, "Leave this house right now and get Sandy a ring." And I was like, "What?" And she said, "There are two different stores you can go to. Go!" So I went to a jeweler and got an estate ring and got down on my knee and asked Sandy to marry me in front of my mother, with everybody laughing. It was great.

Sandy: Our wedding was magical. We rented a home in Temecula, California, where Beth's sister lives with her husband Chris and our nephew Michael. Chris filmed the whole thing. We told Michael, "You can't be putting any of this on Facebook or telling the other nieces and nephews," because we'd only invited a few friends and Beth's other sister in Oregon to keep it small. He was the sole representative of his generation. But it was special because he'd been so supportive. The home was on five acres of land, with a swimming pool and an orange grove. Hot air balloons sailed by every morning. The day of our wedding, we told the flower girl Janet (Beth's college roommate) to "Just go pick some flowers for a bouquet."

Beth: For the rehearsal, we had shirts made that read: "Best Woman," "Flower Girl, "Sister of the Bride," etc. Our shirts said "I'm the Bride and So is She." We got more dressed up for the real deal. To officiate, we found a Unitarian Universalist pastor online who had celebrated many gay and lesbian marriages. We met her in California before leaving for Costa Rica to discuss how we wanted it to be. She was very nice and interviewed us about our history and relationship, and gave a great little speech during the ceremony. Except she forgot to ask us to say the vows we'd written, and we forgot to say them because we were a wreck! In the middle of our catered dinner, Sandy and I stood up and said, "We realized that we didn't get to share our vows earlier, so we're going to share them with you now." Everyone at the table started telling stories—little vignettes about us. It was such an incredible evening.

Sandy: Beth's sister Julie gave a beautiful toast that brought us to tears. I wish that I had a copy of that. She just said it from her heart.

Beth: I've been to a lot of weddings in my lifetime, and they're fine—but it's different when it's your turn to declare your love in front of friends and family. I saw things differently and why it adds love to the world when you say it outloud.

Sandy: I understand people in a relationship who don't want to get married, too. But for us, at the beginning of the ceremony we had a sage stick and a black rock, which are important symbols for us, and four candles that we lit to represent our parents who couldn't be there. It was just a very special moment and I'm glad we did it.

Beth: Of course, now we forget all the time that we're actually married. My sister Barb will send us text messages about something going on here, and when I ask her, "How did you know that?" she says, "Your wife told me." That term still surprises me. I guess we'll always feel like life partners.

Sandy: Marriage is a "standing up"—a public declaration of sorts. At least that was our intention in getting married. Not that I've been very closeted; I've always been very tell-the-truth-and-what-you-think. We don't advertise with a "Lesbians" sign in our yard, but we wear our rings, and people usually ask a little after meeting us, "So how long have you been together?" It's just pretty clear that we love each other. We live in a very conservative county in the mountains of Colorado, and we've lived here for 35 years. People know us as a couple and they respect us because they know what we've done: both in building our own place and who we've helped. My attitude right now is, *This is* *who we are; get over it.* For people who think they don't like gay people, I'm going to be that little crack in the wall that says, "Maybe it is okay. Maybe all these people aren't too weird."

Beth: We have the same cares and responsibilities as any other couple. I'm playful and bring the humor. I'm also the better cook. Sandy is organized. I follow her lists. She does the taxes and she's the deep thinker.

Sandy: We just complement each other in so many ways. Building our art studio this summer is a good example. I'm older now and I don't have much arm strength left to use the nail gun, so I did a lot of the drawing and planning. We both think and figure things out and look it up online when we forget how to do a birdsmouth on the rafters.

Beth: It's hard to separate. We try not to finish each other's sentences though. I hate that.

Sandy: We're also inspired by other couples' examples, even some we don't know personally. Like Edith Windsor, the woman who won the lawsuit to undo DOMA. She and Thea had been a couple together for years and years, over 40, and after Thea passed away, Edith was hit with a huge inheritance tax bill, which she then challenged in court. The tax wasn't fair, so I certainly respected their relationship and how they took care of each other. They were radical women back in the day. They had traveled abroad and participated in protests in New York City and they had done a lot of outrageous things that I thought were cool. I also respect and admire my parents' relationship. My dad died so young that my memories of him are dim, but he and my mom had a good relationship. I respect any couple that dedicated to each other.

Beth: I would also say I respect my parents' marriage, but it's truer in hindsight—now that I'm older and can see how they worked together. That's what any relationship is: you each have your strengths, and you let them be there for the other person.

Sandy: You're lucky if you find that special person in your life. But I also think there can be more than one person in your lifetime. Maybe that's why some marriages don't work—because something happens in a lifetime and you move onto the next person. I don't know, because it hasn't happened to us. When Beth and I were first together, I remember us saying, "We're in this for as long as it's good for both us and works for both of us." So far, it's still good and it still works. Beth will come to me around 10:00 in the morning and say, "Have I told you yet today how much I love you?" It means a lot to me. We're a team and we just try to keep having fun. I think our relationship has been so successful because we both love to learn and we get excited sharing learnings with each other, and that's showing love.

Beth: We do little things for each other. Give hugs. We try and sleep in the same bed together to touch every once in a while. You hear people talking about not squeezing the toothpaste right and I could care less about toothpaste, but I do get annoyed when she leaves water in the sink after doing the dishes. But then I think to myself, *Why do you care? Just pull the* *plug, Beth*. So I'm always like, *Do you really want to spend your energy on that?* We're not perfect; I don't know what perfect would be. Lots of times when we start fighting we're laughing by the end because we see how stupid it is.

Sandy: As our friend Cassie would say, "I'd much rather have Beth mad at me than Sandy, because Beth just yells and walks around slamming doors and then it's over. And Sandy takes a little longer." It's true that I get quiet and pissy for a while. But I'm trying to work on it. We've only been together forty-odd years; we're still working on it. You have to stop and question, *Why am I so invested in my position on this?* and sometimes you realize it's just you being stubborn. I know because I always miss Beth when she's gone. Then I try to show love for her by doing things that we've wanted to get done. Like this last time, I remodeled the pantry. Or Beth will go out and pick up all the lawn chairs and put them away because winter's coming and it's something we need to do. Those things are always appreciated.

Beth: We also write really good cards to each other. Usually Sandy does something with a photograph she's taken and I draw something. We keep all those cards.

Sandy: I'm really not big on material possessions, so cards are the perfect gift. Although—Beth gave me my first iPad and I'm very happy with it and attached to it. One year she made me a sculpture. The things we say to or make for each other are precious.

Beth: In 2014, we sold the ranch ... the hardest thing we've ever had to do. We loved all 72 acres of that land, and knew every inch of it. We loved the house we built and the shared experiences with friends and family who visited over the years. The ranch was like a piece of art that we worked on every day. After we left the ranch, we traveled a while but eventually came back to the area that felt like home. We bought a small house on a river. We looked at all the stuff we'd put in storage and wondered, *Why?* There's still a lot of crap we need to get rid of, but we're ready to pare down. We want to be able to just pick up and go on the next adventure whenever it calls. I got a new pair of snow boots yesterday, and even that seemed extravagant. But I'll need them when we head to the Northwest later this year. We're going to revisit some of the places we went on that summer trip in '76!

Sandy: We try to plan special trips around our anniversary every year. We don't always make it a really big deal—sometimes we just go to dinner here in the mountains—but we often take a trip to a place that we love, like Santa Fe. No matter where we are, we do pause and feel thankful for another trip around the sun together. Travel and health: those are the biggies. So long as we have those—and health has got to come first before travel—then we have everything we need. I've got to get rid of this Lyme disease so I can do things again. I've been on treatment for 4 months now and just started working with a doctor in Idaho who uses a different approach, so I'm feeling positive.

Beth: After we sold the ranch and we didn't know what we were doing, just traveling around in the camper for

Beth & Sandy

a while, we adopted the mantra "It shall be revealed." We realized that we'd been wasting all this time thinking we knew what we were doing and where we were going, but we didn't—because everything's always changing. It's been nice, taking the stress, the ego out of living. So: travel, yes, and I think we both want to do more art. It gives us good energy.

Sandy: And plants. That's the future: continue to learn, continue to do, continue to help others.

2018

Beth: I was riding with Janet, my college roommate, the other day and we drove past a senior housing complex. They still had some *Hilary for President* signs up in their windows and I said, "Look, Janet—cool people! You know that's us now."

Sandy: We're noticing now that people our age are considered 'old.' We want to write a book about it: *The Invisibles*. All about how once you get to be a certain age, people don't even see you anymore.

Beth: I guess it's time for us to go to an assisted living facility.

Sandy: Or buy a blueberry farm ...

[Both start laughing.]

Beth: Yeah, one or the other!

"

This is my king, Justin. We're at our engagement ceremony here—also known as the 'traditional wedding' in Yoruba culture. Each family has a color. My family's color is blue; Justin's family's color is red. I'm wearing red in this photo to symbolize that I'm joining his family.

—Toni (31)
Dentist

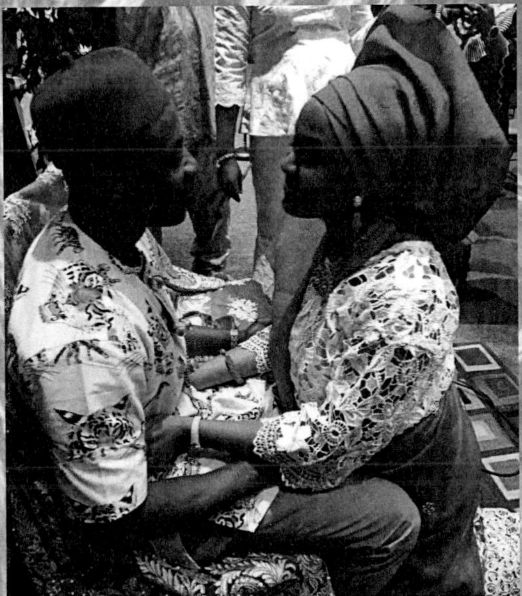

“

[from *Fates and Furies*]

They had been married for seventeen years; she lived in the deepest room in his heart. And sometimes that meant that wife occurred to him before Mathilde, helpmeet before herself. Abstraction of her before the visceral being. But not now. When she came across the veranda, he saw Mathilde all of a sudden. The dark whip at the center of her. How, so gently, she flicked it and kept him spinning.

—Lauren Groff (39)
Author

AFTERWORD: DR. ALLISON SALLEE

[C2 Change is a 501(c)(3) nonprofit organization dedicated to providing quality mental health treatment to Austin families regardless of income. Their motto is: "We treat the WHOLE family, so that treatment is faster, more effective, and longer lasting." Proceeds from the sale of OF TNY THREADS *benefit C2 Change.]*

I returned to school in 1994 and subsequently became a licensed psychologist and a licensed marriage and family therapist. For many years, I had the dream of creating a place where people could come for help with their problems and not be turned away because of a lack of funds or because their insurance wouldn't pay for it. I had no idea what I was doing, but I saved up $10,000 over the course of several years, and in 2010 rented the tiny office next to mine. Thus began this attempt to offer our community the services that I knew we needed.

My passion was truly fueled by the many people with whom I had worked over the years. They were so hard-working, so grateful for the help, and had so many barriers to access. The stories are many and some are heartbreaking. I have worked with families that were forced into ridiculously high deductibles for mental health services (i.e., thousands of dollars annually), or who were denied such services because their insurance declined to provide coverage for, say, autism. Then there were those who were working three jobs in self-employed capacities, such as a janitor, who couldn't afford private insurance.

There were families whose schools refused to test their children for learning disorders or intellectual disabilities, and one family whose principal shredded the documentation of the child's learning disorder results (yes, it happened to many families and the principal was fired, but in the meantime the child went almost a full school year without services). There are stories of families whose physicians refused to sign documents proving the child was developmentally delayed so that the family could get in-home help. In one case, a mother showed up with bruises to her face and arms because her child was much bigger than she, and nonverbal, had used physical aggression to communicate. There were also women who wanted to get out of abusive relationships or recover from them.

I remember speaking to an insurance adjuster once who asked, "What's so terrible about an abusive relationship that someone would actually need therapy?" Another time, family members lost a loved one to suicide, and again, an adjuster asked me what was so terrible about the death that it would actually require therapy. I've worked with families who have adult children with autism, yet were forced by insurance companies to have another evaluation to prove the adult child has autism so that he could stay on his parents' health insurance plan. In the meantime, the family had to pay out of pocket for the evaluation because it was not medically necessary.

I have worked with families who had a partner get cancer, and begin treatment for the cancer, only to lose their job because they could not work during part of the treatment. They went on to rack up tens of thousands of dollars in medical costs.

The stories go on and on. In the end, I simply wanted to help these families who needed mental health services, wanted them, and deserved them.

My hope was to help the whole family. Having worked with children and families for a number of years, I was always struck by the fact that in our community, so many therapists would work with just one member of the family (i.e., the child or one partner of the coupleship). Training in Austin focused on similar approaches. I worked with so many people who would ask, "What do I do when my child/my partner/etc. does ... ?" I wanted to create a place that brought people together. I think that is what most humans want: to be together in a meaningful way.

We have two aspirations at C2 Change: to serve couples, and to serve families with children. Couples are the foundation for families. They are families. Each individual is the rock on which the other partner can rely; together, they become their children's lens to the world, and their children's emotional barometer. We serve children and adolescents because they are our future; because we can help prevent some of the things that happen in the future when people don't get help early; and because children and adolescents often have no choice, no voice. Our approach is preventative.

In starting a center that could be a place for so many, I also wanted to create space to train new clinicians who could work with couples and children with families. In this way, we would not only be helping those in need now, but we would be creating future resources for those who will be in need. Our community needs more clinicians who are trained to work systemically. A systemic approach is one that strives to teach family members the tools they need to live successfully and independently together. Our goal is to get families out of our offices and back into their homes. We want to teach them the tools and skills they need to do what they want (versus being dependent on a therapist to sort it out for them forever). This does not mean we do not do long-term work. It just means that we are eager to help people develop themselves and feel less dependent on a therapist for any chance of healing or happiness.

One of our hopes for couples is to provide free premarital workshops through the Twogether in Texas program. Twogether in Texas encourages couples to attend premarital counseling in exchange for a discount on their marriage license fee. The thinking is to help couples start off on the right foot, by teaching them how to build a happy home, lay the foundation for the future, and work in a healthy way through any tough times.

Over the years, my frustration has mounted, and I have (like many) become disenchanted with the broken system we call "health care." This disenchantment was another inspiration for creating a nonprofit center. It's the first time I have ever put this in writing, but as Jessica has so graciously been sharing stories for the benefit of helping others, perhaps it is time. Our health care system, and especially our mental health system, is broken. I know this is not news to you.

What is important to know is that the attempts to make it better are also broken. We continue to operate on a business model that bets human health against the dollar. Insurance is not set up to provide health care. It is set up to make money—understandably. I have no problem with people trying to make a living. I have a problem with the fact that we are using human health as the commodity. Humans will always get sick. We are designed to do so. It's very different from a market that bets on whether or not gold will go up or down in value. The state of human health is a constant, and we are trying to use a for-profit model, paying out shareholders, lining others' pockets by betting on human health and denying care when it becomes unprofitable.

"So," you might say, "this is why we need socialized medicine." I disagree. We have had three major pilot studies of socialized medicine and they have been limited in their success if not unsuccessful: Medicaid, Medicare, and the VA system. In countries that do have socialized medicine, corruption is rampant (my guess is that it's as rampant as in our for-profit model!). Patients are often forced to pay cash to move up on the waitlist for necessary treatments, or, worse, even get on a waitlist. So, this is one reason I decided I had to do something to help others.

I think there may be an answer, or at least a model we have not tried in its entirety. Perhaps a hybrid model of a "not-for-profit" would work. It would still operate within the private sector, but not concern itself with trying to make a profit to pay shareholders. Any profit would go back to the pot, so to speak, and then be used for future claims. It negates the bureaucracy that often comes with socialized medicine and neutralizes the hedging on human health that comes with a for-profit model. Models like this do exist, even here in the U.S. They take the form of small co-ops, like Mutual of Omaha. These companies compile the profits, then pro-rate and distribute them back to members who can use the funds to pay future premiums or pay other bills. Ideally, the profits would benefit those who cannot afford insurance, due to a medical or intellectual disability. Not-for-profit models still require people to pay into the system, so tax payers are not burdened.

Again, my hope was to help families. In the end, I think we are doing this. It is very hard for me to step back and see all that we have done and all that we do. I am always thinking about where I want us to be. But those sweet little moments—the ones where I get a note from a couple who were so thankful for their therapist, or the parents who drove hundreds of miles to get an evaluation, or the family who says "Thank you for what you are doing," or the child who initially could not look me in the eye or bear any touch, but who cried and hugged me goodbye on our last visit—those are the moments that make me think this is a good thing that we are doing.

I hope by reading this, you will be inspired to realize your passion and find a way to support it. There are lots of good things happening and nonprofits need you.

We are so grateful to Jessica Hagemann for her passion to tell untellable tales and for her desire to help nonprofits raise funds through book proceeds. Proceeds from the sales of this book will go toward funding our Twogether in Texas program to help local couples begin their lives together with evidence-based, real-life tools for successful relationships.

ACKNOWLEDGMENTS

Simon, Julie, Prabin, Jade, Morgana, Ellen, Robert, Katie, Reigh, Shenal, Lindsay, Adam, Jenna, Beth, and Sandy: thank you for so selflessly sharing your stories. This book is powerful because you were honest. You remind the rest of us how to love.

Brendan Owens and Dr. Allison Sallee: by letting me inside your walls and entrusting me with your clients' and employees' stories, you lived your mission "To make the world a better place, one family at a time." Thank you for the important work you do.

Cafe Ruckus, Whichcraft, Fat Cats, Cherrywood Coffeehouse, and Schlotzsky's Deli: you didn't know that I was picking apart the inner workings of human romantic relationships in your booths while drinking your coffee, but thank you after the fact for providing safe, clean, and accessible public meeting spaces.

THREADS was made possible thanks to the generous donations of many individuals and organizations, who either gave monetary gifts or otherwise funded the publication of this book by purchasing POSTMARKS ON OUR FOREHEADS (Book I in the *Untellable Tales* series) and/or WHISPERS: HEALING & TRIUMPH AFTER SEXUAL ASSAULT (Book II).

To Brandon Bross at Forty Acres Press: your mad printing skills never fail to amaze.

Tiara Marshall: as usual, you nailed the cover art!

John Hagemann: the text of this book would not be as tight without your sharp eye and editorial skills.

Tal Leeds, Kate Lee, Caleb Heine, and Justine Harrington assisted Cider Spoon's interview transcription efforts.

OF TINY THREADS: STORIES ABOUT AMERICAN MARRIAGE is dedicated to my good friends and neighbors, David and Emily Tietz. May you always be as happy together as you are right now.

ABOUT THE PROJECT

OF TINY THREADS: STORIES ABOUT AMERICAN MARRIAGE is the third book in Cider Spoon's *Untellable Tales* series. Each *Untellable Tales* book compiles the stories of a distinct demographic whose stories need to be heard, but that we as a society aren't talking about enough. All proceeds from *Untellable Tales* book sales benefit Austin nonprofit organizations working in a related field.

Book I, POSTMARKS ON OUR FOREHEADS: HOSPICE CARE PATIENTS, MEMORY CARE PATIENTS, & THE PEOPLE WHO LOVE THEM, was the end result of the 2015 Indiegogo crowdfunding campaign "Help Hospice Patients Write Their Life Stories!" The campaign was organized by Cider Spoon Stories, "Austin's premier ghostwriting service for every story." Ghostwriter and editor Jess Hagemann got the idea for the project after a year spent volunteering with an Austin-based hospice care program. Proceeds from the sale of POSTMARKS benefit Hospice Austin.

Book II, WHISPERS: HEALING & TRIUMPH AFTER SEXUAL ASSAULT, includes the inspiring true stories of ten survivors and two survivor-advocates. Proceeds benefit The SAFE (Stop Abuse for Everyone) Alliance.

Proceeds from the sale of THREADS benefit C2 Change, a nonprofit mental health agency providing free or low-cost marital counseling.

All *Untellable Tales* books are available for purchase on Amazon.com or the Cider Spoon Stories website at www.CiderSpoonStories.com.

Jess Hagemann is an award-winning author and Austin-based ghostwriter. You may contact her at www.ciderspoonstories.com or ciderspoon [at] gmail [dot] com.